Layered Curriculum:

*The practical solution for teachers with
more than one student in their classroom*

D0972861

4th printing
Copyright © 2001, 2002
Kathie F. Nunley, EdD

ISBN 1-929358-08-3

Additional copies of this book as well as all books and guides by
Kathie F. Nunley are available at:
http://Help4Teachers.com

For information on workshops and other presentations visit:
http://help4teachers.com
or Email: Kathie@brains.org

Cover Design by Micheal R. Eudy
Eudy Animation   Dallas, Texas

Printed in the USA by Morris Publishing
3212 East Highway 30
Kearney, NE 68847

Acknowledgments

So many people have assisted me in the writing of this book. I must thank my wonderfully supportive husband and patient children. And a big thanks to my colleagues and fellow teachers who have been so willing to share their thoughts, opinions, and creative minds.

This book is dedicated to my mother.

Like teaching, mothering is often a thankless job. When we are young, we do not recognize the need to say thank you. When we are old enough, we seldom take the time to go back.

Table of Contents

The suspense is terrible . . . I hope it'll last. - Willy Wonka

Chapter One

Santa don't come to the Projects

Teaching is one of the great joys of life. Our interaction with young people is an experience like no other. I think it is what calls us back to the classroom each year.

For each year is a new beginning, a renewed opportunity to touch the future through young minds. But with the power that lies in our position comes a great responsibility. There must be constant reflection on our methods and philosophies. For although we strive to make a difference and improve the lives of the children, above all else, we should do no harm.

I love to teach. Teaching is an art which takes advantage of creativity. My views on education, philosophies of instruction, and teaching methods have been evolving with every school year. Life events both in and out of school create the lens through which I view this profession.

My teaching career began in the inner-city schools of a low socio-economic region in the south. Teaching to this 98% African-American low SES population made for some creative opportunities.

These are schools where every teacher used an overhead projector so that you never turned your back on the class. I was introduced to teaching in a highly secure facility.

I was particularly influenced by an experience I had teaching a pilot program for illiterate males repeating science for the third time. These repeated failures were a fascinating bunch who eventually referred to themselves as the "Nunley Boys". This group of children, ranging in age from 15 to 18, were the equivalent to the *sweat hogs* of our community. Disliked, feared and basically unloved, this group comprised my fourth period general biology class. Other teachers would ask me if I was frightened to have all these boys together in one class. I would chuckle and shake my head at their ignorance. What they didn't understand or know was the safety and love shared by this special population.

One of the first eye-openers came near Thanksgiving when the topic of Santa Claus came up. One of the students piped up with "Ms. Nunley, don't you know Santa don't come to the Projects?"

"What do you mean, Santa doesn't come?" I naively asked.

They then began to tell me the stories that their mothers and grandmothers had given for why Santa didn't come to their homes on Christmas eve. Until that moment I had never thought what it must be like to raise a child in this culture where Santa is everywhere and promises to bring things, but on Christmas morning, the story brings nothing but disappointment.

"My mother told me 'Santa is too scared to come to the Projects.'"

"Grandma told me 'Santa's sleigh got hit by a plane'".

"When I was eight years old, I asked Santa for a bike and he said he'd bring it, so I told all my friends I was gettin' a bike. They didn't believe me, but I kept sayin', 'yep, Santa told me'. Then on Christmas morning, I looked, but no bike. All my friends say, 'so where's your new bike?' I just said, 'Oh, it's at my grandma's' or 'Oh, my brother's ridin it' or make up somethin' til they quit askin'".

By the end of the period, I was fighting back tears.

The next day, we made Christmas stockings. I had construction paper, glitter, glue, string, etc. and they had to make a stocking - no arguments. I told them it was an assignment and they had to decorate it with the various kingdoms of life. They grumbled and groaned, but they each made a stocking which we hung in the chalk tray at the front of the room. I told them that Santa might not come to the Housing Projects, but he did sometimes come to schools.

Everyday, there was something in their stockings. It wasn't much, maybe just a home-made cookie or a little candy sucker, but something was there. Then a funny thing started to happen. The boys started coming up with excuses to come in to the classroom early in the morning.

Karl might wander in with "Ms. Nunley, mind if I leave my backpack in here til class?"

"Sure", I'd say, "that's fine".

So Karl would saunter in. You have to picture this big, tall, gang member who lives on the street as often as in a home, coming in with the appropriate machismo bounce in his walk, tossing the backpack behind my desk, then muttering, " Well, 'long as I'm here, might as well check the stocking". In a little while here would come another one, with his excuse for entering the room and checking his stocking. Sometimes they'd show up with cuts, and bumps because they knew I had a first aid kit and would help them clean it and bandage it. Sometimes they'd come in for a peanut butter sandwich in the morning because they knew there was always bread and peanut butter in the cabinet.

One day Bobby came from his cooking class with something wrapped in foil which he tossed on my desk.

"Is this for me?" I asked.

"Yeah, whatever," he'd mumble, looking at his shoes. Then, "Oh, man, I almost forgot" as he reached into his back pocket for the fork which he set by the foil.

He had made me a pizza. It was the worst looking piece of pizza you had ever seen in your life, but you better believe I ate it all, with delight.

Going to "the outside"

We talked about state parks and areas surrounding our city. One day I jokingly mentioned that if they all passed the course that semester, we'd all go on a camping trip to a state park just across the state line, "the outside" as they called it. Well, you guessed it, they all passed and they held me to my promise. After a discussion with my principal, we decided that a week-end camping trip to the park would be feasible with some help from the community. The local newspaper came out and did a story, took a picture of the class and everything. Those boys were so thrilled to see themselves on the front page for something non-criminal. We got a few calls from people horrified that my principal would "let some white woman go off into the woods with a bunch of black boys!" but most calls were supportive and the donations came flooding in. We had tents, sleeping bags and enough food for an army. The trip was a success. Several other teachers (male and female) volunteered to come along. The rules were simple - no guns, no drugs. The boys understood. We roasted marshmallows, rented canoes, pitched tents and listened to bird calls. The boys were on *the outside*.

You must build a relationship of trust before you can have a teaching-learning relationship. Few, if any of these children had homes. Most had criminal records, some serious. I visited with more of their parol officers than parents. People feared them. They were unloved. And that - was their greatest problem. I learned that every child needed to be loved. A kind word, a safe place, a peanut butter sandwich when you're hungry. These are basic needs.

So when those other teachers inquired with whispers in the hallway, "Aren't you scared to death to have all those boys in one room?" I knew the real answer was that it was the safest place on earth. Those boys would never harm me. In fact, they would kill for me (I'm afraid that may be literally). I still wonder about those boys, Karl, Bobby, Duck, Clarence and the others, and miss them terribly. I hope I taught them half as much as they taught me.

Every Child deserves a Special Education

I am a regular education teacher and a special education parent. In addition to my teaching and research, I am the mother of four children. My oldest child is 16 year old son Keegan. Keegan has autism. Although he has what is termed very high-functioning autism, raising Keegan has probably been the single most important influence on my educational philosophies.

From Keegan I have learned not to take learning for granted. What many of us learn through everyday modeling, some have to learn through direct instruction. From Keegan I have also learned the importance of letting all students have an equal chance to learn. No one wants to feel singled out or special due to a disability. He has also taught me to never underestimate the potential of special ed students.

I also have a beautiful 12 year old daughter. In addition to teaching me important points about teen heartthrobs and music, I have learned from her about brain plasticity. She has been recovering from a depressed skull fracture since her first birthday. A head-on collision with a drunk driver resulted in damage to the frontal lobes of her brain and an immediate loss in her speech and hearing.

Watching her recovery from the brain-damage has taught me a great deal about the brain's ability to accommodate, rearrange and redesign. This ability is known as brain plasticity.

When the damage to her brain resulted in her losing both her speech and her hearing, we were forced to start her in public education at the age of 13 months. The infant stimulation program was miraculous and today my daughter speaks and hears like any other 12 year old. Since the parts of her brain responsible for speaking and hearing were damaged, other areas were trained to perform those functions. The recovery was so successful that today she attends a school for gifted and talented students.

I also have a seven year old son, who was our first child to enter into "regular education" - a real eye opener for my husband who is still nervous that there is no IEP and you just have to take "pot-luck" when it comes to classes, teachers and instruction. It's hard to explain why every student is not entitled to a special education.

Last, but not least is my three year old son, who, by nature of being three, would be considered in need of special education. Actually he is especially delightful for me to watch at this juncture in my life as I now have a stronger background in brain development and I delight in watching his neurons bloom with dendrites nearly before my eyes.

Mankind should be our business Ebenezer, but it seldom is.
                                        — Jacob Marlee

Chapter Two

The Evolution of Layered Curriculum

The idea for Layered Curriculum began in the late 1980's when I first took a look at the learning styles work being done primarily with Rita Dunn and her associates. I think learning styles was the first time that education "came out of the closet" so to speak and openly acknowledged that one size does not fit all. This came at a critical time in education when desegregation and the inclusion mandates from the 1970's had been around long enough to generate a bushel of problems.

America had come to terms with the flagrant discrimination which had occurred in schools. They saw how tracking was too often a smoke screen for segregation, that separate but equal was not necessarily so. Research was showing that students benefitted most from heterogenous classrooms and parents were demanding that segregation for color, disability and language be eliminated.

Teachers were finding that the old stand and deliver methods that had been used in their building for generations were failing. For the first time, teachers were asked to teach to a wide variety of abilities, cultures and languages. If America was truly going to educate the masses, something had to change.

Learning styles was one of the first serious looks at how education would have to address these changes. Teachers began looking at the physical, social and emotional differences and needs of children. Suddenly teachers and administrators starting looking seriously at issues such as time of day, light, dietary needs, classroom furniture, material and arrangement, and instructional strategies. Unfortunately, architects were not looking at learning styles during this period and we were left with many new schools with windowless classrooms. But that's a different chapter.

To get back to my original topic, the evolution of Layered Curriculum, I believe it started when I first looked at various learning styles models and they intrigued me. At that point I "played around" with the teaching techniques for a few years and found them quite valuable and necessary.

I was satisfied in my journey toward accommodating learning styles until another brilliant mind came along and re-directed my thinking. A man by the name of Howard Gardner introduced to me the idea of multiple intelligences. Gardner's work pointed out how education was spending too much time speaking to the logical and linguistic intelligent child and too little time directed toward children with other strengths, e.g.: the musical or interpersonal intelligences. I looked at Gardner's work too, and realized that it had significant importance to this new and varied classroom.

About the time that I tried to inter-play multiple intelligence with learning styles, I was struck by another voice in education — Anthony Gregorc. Tony Gregorc introduced me to "Mind Styles". Gregorc's work illustrated 4 styles of the mind, concrete sequential, concrete random, abstract sequential, abstract random. He was able to graphically show me the problems encountered when an abstract random minded child finds his way into a concrete sequential minded teacher's classroom. Children who can't function sequentially often find themselves in the vice-principal's office. On the other hand, one also has to feel empathy for the concrete sequential child trying to outline a lecture given by the free thinking abstract random teacher. I looked at Gregorc's work too, and realized its importance in education.

To add more worries to my dilemma was the realization that someone had put special education children in my room. And they just kept coming. The growth in special education has been exponential. *Inclusion, Mainstreaming* and *Least Restrictive Environment* were creeping into the vocabulary of the regular ed teacher. The problem was that no one had prepared us for their coming nor told us what to do with them when they arrived.

Thus, I came to two conclusions- Number one: Although I am considered a *regular educator* there are no *regular students*. Number two: Every student deserves a special education.

Where are the Regular Students in Regular Education?

Since the 1970's the numbers of students in special education have increased by 400 percent. The numbers are so high, that the ratio is now seven to one. In other words, for every eight children in this country in public education, one is a special education student.

Where did this sudden increase come from? It's not because people are suddenly giving birth in large numbers to children with disabilities. In fact, the numbers of birth defects have been going down as pre-natal care has gone up. There are three main reasons for the increase in special education numbers.

First, instruments psychologists and school districts use to detect disabilities have become more sophisticated. We are now able to identify disabilities or risk of disability sooner.

Secondly, parents are better informed. They understand what services their children are entitled to and they are organized enough to work the system and get those services. Parent support and advocacy groups are strong, powerful and effective.

Thirdly, and most significantly, we as a nation have become more compassionate. If you look at disabilities as an event on a continuum, you will see that we are all disabled to some extent. It's just a matter of drawing a line somewhere on the continuum and then declaring that everyone on the left is disabled, everyone on the right, is not. As the years go on, we keep moving the line. Basically the emotion of the country asks that we include just a few more, and just a few more, and so on, until the line on the continuum has moved a significant distance and we have a lot more people on the left side of that line than we used to.

This movement reflects itself in the general classroom. The regular education teacher is finding himself faced with increasing diversity and fewer and fewer "regular" students. In fact one might say there are no "regular" students in regular education.

If we look at a typical classroom of 32 students, we will find four students who have been officially identified by the special education system. These are students who have individualized education plans (**IEP's**) with written modifications that must be made to their instruction. In some cases the regular classroom teacher has been informed of these modifications, but frequently they have not. Despite federal law which mandates that all people involved in the education of a student be informed of the modifications and have access to the IEP, many schools leave the regular education teacher completely in the dark.

In the same classroom, you have another four students I call the *unidentified special education students*. These are students who should be identified as special education students but are not. These children have either thus far escaped the attention of the special ed department or, as is often the case at the secondary level, these are students who once were in special education, but have dropped out. Often students will go through elementary school in special ed, but once they hit junior or senior high, they don't want the stigma associated with being in special education.

Special education is not the only source of diversity and challenge in the regular classroom. In addition to the special education students, the typical classroom will also have two students with an attention deficit disorder, and two who do not speak English as their native language. Obviously, depending on your community, these numbers may be much higher. Attention deficit disorder tends to run in families, so depending on where you teach, you may have a far greater number of ADD or ADHD students in the room.

In this same widely mixed classroom, you are also trying to accommodate a variety of learning styles. The classroom will contain about eight visual learners, seven auditory learners, and 18 tactile learners who learn best by manipulating material.

The tactile learners are generally the ones who present the greatest challenge to teachers. Designing instructional strategies for tactile learners is difficult for most teachers because that is not our learning style. Teachers, for the most part, are visual and auditory learners. We know this because teachers have all successfully completed college. And college screens for the visual and auditory learner.

Accommodating the needs of this tremendously diverse group is no small task for the regular education teacher. How do we modify instruction for all these students? In the past, we've been asked to make individual modifications based on suggestions by the resource or special education teacher. These may have included things like highlighting important ideas in the textbook, having peer tutors, reducing class and homework assignments for specific students, etc.

There are serious problems with individual modifications. First, these individual modifications are tremendously overwhelming to the regular education teacher. In addition to the wide demands put on a teacher in a large diverse classroom population, this additional request was often overlooked or done sporadically at best.

The second, and probably most significant problem with individual modification is that it is extremely stigmatizing to the student. Regardless of how discreet you may be in individualizing modifications, the student knows they have a "special program" as does the rest of the class. The most common reason for students dropping out of special education, particularly at the secondary level, is the stigma attached to special education.

In addition to overwhelming the teacher and stigmatizing the learner, individual modifications have created grading nightmares. The issue always arises about *fairness*. Is it fair to give the same grade to a student who has been assigned only half the math problems as the student who has done them all?

Out of this mix of inclusion, stigma, learning styles, multiple intelligences, mind styles and cultural diversity, came the idea for Layered Curriculum.

I could see that the more reasonable solution to successfully including all types of learners was to modify the entire curriculum rather than make individual accommodation. These so called *whole-class* curriculum modifications make inclusion and teaching in the regular classroom so much more enjoyable. The method I designed and have used for several years in my own classroom is a method I now call Layered Curriculum.

Layered Curriculum is so named because the entire curriculum is presented to students in three layers. Each layer represents a different depth of study in a topic or unit of learning. Students can choose how deep they wish to examine a topic and thereby choose their own grade as well.

Layered Curriculum is based on a triangular shaped learning model. The bottom layer is the largest, covers general content, and is basically designed around meeting my state's core curriculum and preparing my students for state mandated exams. The middle layer is smaller and asks student to apply concepts learned in the bottom layer. The top layer is the smallest and requires a higher critical thinking assignment of students.

As I'll discuss in detail later, Layered Curriculum uses a different paradigm for grading as well. I designed Layered Curriculum with the idea in mind that I wanted a grade to mean something. Rather than the traditional grading system based on a percent of information recalled, the grading in Layered Curriculum reflects the student's chosen depth of study. The higher the grade, the deeper understanding a student has demonstrated.

The design is one of a completely student-centered classroom which focuses learning on the student and allows the teacher the role of facilitator. The following chapters will focus on each level, called layers, defining its purpose, design and grading.

Chapter Three

The Bottom Layer-- The C level

The bottom layer is called the **"C" level** because the highest grade a student can receive by working solely in this layer is the grade of "C". This is the fattest layer with the most assignment choices. The level provides an opportunity for students to get a general understanding of the topic. The "C" level asks the student to collect factual information on a topic in a learning style, reading level, and language which is most comfortable to him or her.

The "C" level is constructed by offering approximately 15 -20 assignments choices. The choices are designed to collect information on the unit's particular topic of study. The assignments are presented in a written form on what is called *a unit sheet*.

These "C" level assignments will include choices for *visual learners*. Assignments appropriate here would be textbook readings and questions, videos to watch, magazine and newspaper articles to summarize. Demonstrations, computer programs and art projects would also be appropriate for visual learners.

The "C" level also includes assignments for *auditory learners*. These assignments might include audio-taped lectures or readings, live lecture and discussion groups as well as videos. Students with ADD/ADHD seem to enjoy taped lectures which they can listen to with headsets. The headsets help block out other distractions.

The bulk of the assignments in the "C" level are for *tactile learners*. Remembering that in most general classrooms, they make up the majority of learners, don't skimp on these assignments. Many of the assignments given for visual and auditory learners may include tactile learners as well. Appropriate assignments here would be art posters using various mediums, models, clay sculptures, drawings, computer work, flash cards, or vocabulary string boards, mobiles and dioramas. Tactile assignments are particularly important if you have students who are poor readers or students with limited English proficiency.

In addition to addressing the needs of various learning styles, the "C" level should include one or two assignments that can be done in a language other than English. These may include a written report or summary on a lecture, video, or even previous knowledge. The importance here is to allow self-efficacy in your English as a Second Language (*ESL*) students. An unexpected advantage I found to these ESL assignments was with students I have who are first generation American. These students can speak their native tongue, but often cannot write in it, but their parents can. I find students asking if they can take the assignment home, work with their parents and have their parents write the assignment which they would then bring back and read. This was a wonderful opportunity to involve cross-cultural families in school and homework activities.

Right about now is when teachers start to seriously wonder how I'm going to grade all this! We'll get to that (the best part) in a minute.

One of the most important things you can do in a Layered Curriculum classroom is to use a wide *variety of textbooks* and reading sources rather than the traditional classroom set of books. In my general biology classroom I may have 25 different biology textbooks. I have some at a college reading level, many at various high school level and some general science books written at an elementary level. This same idea holds for all the reading material. So although I get the newspaper, *Time* and *Scientific American*, I also get *Ranger Rick* and occasionally, *My Big Backyard*. This way I'm assured of having something at a reading level for everyone. This also provides "reading material" for non-readers.

Each assignment is worth a certain number of points based on the difficulty of the assignment and how much time it requires. Students will not do all the assignments, but rather, choose several to accumulate the number of points they want. There are a minimum amount of points required as well as a maximum. Students may not accumulate more points than a "C" worth.

Remember, this level is designed for general collection of information. Students are free to search for and gather a wide variety of information pertaining to the unit. You may want to involve the students in designing assignments, especially later in the year as students become familiar with Layered Curriculum.

Grading the "C" level

The grading is the best part of Layered Curriculum. All assignments at the "C" level are graded through an **oral defense**. At first glance, this may appear to be an overwhelming task, but is actually easily managed. This is the key facilitation role of the teacher. When students complete an assignment I simply ask them a few questions about what they've learned. It takes about a minute to assess whether or not learning has actually taken place.

Be prepared, at first, this will be a shock to your students. Many have come through years of school never realizing that the point of an assignment was to learn something. For most of them, they thought the goal of an assignment was to just "do" it. If they got something down on a sheet of paper, put their name on top and turned it in, that was it - credit given. The idea of actually learning something from the activity probably has never occurred to them. This realization on my part was what fueled my idea for oral defense.

I do give them fair notice of this. At the first of the year, I explain the Layered Curriculum model to them thoroughly. They know that they will only get credit for learning something, not for simply doing an assignment. This still may be a point of serious adjustment on the part of the student for the first several weeks.

This critical part of Layered Curriculum is a complete shift in thinking on the part of student and teachers. No credit is given for "doing" an assignment. Credit is only earned through learning. How one learns is not important.

For example, in my classroom, textbook questions are worth 15 points. To grade this assignment, I simply pick up the questions, choose three at random to ask, and the student earns five points for each question he answers correctly. I may ask for clarification or a different explanation on any question to make sure the student understands what he is talking about. If two students worked together on the assignment I may do the assessment separately or together as a discussion with students adding to their classmate's response. The point here is to see what learning has taken place.

Flash card vocabulary assignments are worth 10 points. I take the flash cards, choose 10 at random and ask the student the words. He gets a point each. So if he gets four words correct he has the choice of getting four points or getting his flash cards back to study further. In the beginning you get a lot of "you mean I did all those for nothing?" types of questions. My response would be "If you learned nothing from it, then it *was* all for nothing." Regardless of how wonderful the flash cards look, how colorful and pretty, the credit comes from learning the vocabulary - that was the point of the assignment. One student can make flash cards and then all his friends are welcome to use them. That's no problem, because here again, the point is to learn the vocabulary, not make pretty flash cards.

The bulk of my class time is spent in this type of dialogue. After a brief lecture and time for students to get their materials, I begin in one corner of the room and work my way around in a sequential manner, stopping to check on each student. I facilitate, direct, encourage, and grade completed assignments. As I am grading individuals, everyone else continues to work on their own assignments.

There are so many benefits to oral assessment that one has to actually try it to truly understand the difference. The first benefit is that it is generally a less stressful type of assessment than a formal exam. Since stress is one of the biggest suppressors of memory retrieval, most students benefit from alternative testing strategies. An informal discussion with the teacher often allows them to convey what they have truly learned and any new thoughts generated on a topic.

Oral assessment also allows the teacher to really understand whether students are understanding a topic or whether it is time to go back and review.

I remember the years when I gave written formal tests to my general biology classes. I would work so hard on designing the exam, but was always disappointed with how few students actually studied for it. Many would simply guess at the multiple choice and leave all the free response questions blank. Even the comments I wrote on the tests during correction were seldom read. I found that the time span between test and results was often too long to be meaningful. With face-to-face dialogue I don't encounter these problems. I can immediately correct errors, I can encourage deeper thought and explanation and I can help tie together the idea of class assignments and learning. Eventually students actually start asking themselves before they begin an assignment, "What I am supposed to be learning from this?" What an exciting difference.

The biggest benefit of oral assessment is the joy of teaching. Many teachers haven't given much thought as to why they enjoy teaching, but I'll bet it's not because they love parent-teacher conference or filling out attendance records. The real joy of teaching comes from building relationships with wonderful young people and hoping that just one thing you say today will make a difference or ignite a spark in one mind. When you visit every day with every student you magnify the opportunity for this joy of teaching.

As I mentioned in the first chapter, relationship building is critical in the learning experience. So often, especially in large secondary schools, students come to school, go through six or seven periods, go home at the end of the day, and no one has even acknowledged their presence. For many children simply getting up, dressed and arriving on time is a big accomplishment, given the homes and family situations they are living in. How tragic that we can allow that effort to go unrecognized. So if only to say "welcome, thanks for coming, I'm so glad you're here", oral assessment is a good thing. As I move around my classroom, checking on the progress and work of students, I visit with everyone. It allows me to have some sort of exchange, no matter how small, with every student, every day.

"C" level assignment suggestions for visual learners

Here are some suggestions for types of activities and assignment choices that would be found in a "C" level.

Textbooks

- Read the chapter.
- Read and summarize.
- Read and answer the questions at the end.
- Read and be prepared to answer the questions at the end.
- Read and be prepared to explain any illustration.
- Read the chapter and take a publisher-made quiz.

Magazines articles

- Read the article and give me a 60 second summary.
- Read the article with a friend, each take an opposing point and debate it.
- Read and write a one paragraph summary of the main idea.
- Read the magazine and answer the worksheet.
- Find a magazine article on this topic. Highlight the key ideas.

Newspaper articles

- Read the article and give me a summary, written or oral.
- Find a newspaper article on this topic, highlight the important points.
- Find a newspaper article, clip it and give a 60 second summary to the class.

Video

- Watch the video.
- Watch the video and take notes.
- Watch the entire video and write 15 interesting things you learned from it.
- Watch the video and take a quiz at the end.
- Watch the video and fill out the worksheet.

Demonstration

- Watch and contribute to the discussion.
- Watch and then make one of your own.
- Watch the demonstration then use the ideas in one of the labs.
- Watch the demonstration and complete the worksheet.

Computer Program

- Work the program and summarize the key ideas.
- Work the program and fill out the worksheet.
- Work the program and take a quiz at the end.

"C" level assignment suggestions for auditory learners

Taped textbook reading

- Listen to the textbook reading and follow along in the book. Do the end of the chapter questions on paper.
- Listen and follow along with the reading. Do the activities as indicated on the tape.
- Listen and follow along with the reading. Be prepared to orally answer the end of the chapter questions.

Lectures

- Listen to the lecture and take notes.
- Listen to the lecture and fill out the outline.

Debates

- In a group of four, plan a debate. Use at least 3 sources of information for your point and document it. Be prepared to debate on day 4.
- Read the magazine article with a friend. Each of you take a side and debate it. Be prepared to summarize the points of the debate.

Song Writing

- Write a song on (Arthropods). Include at least 10 new facts in the song. Perform it for me or 3 classmates.

"C" level assignment suggestions for tactile learners

Computer programs

- Work the computer program and fill out the worksheet.
- Work the computer program and take the quiz at the end.
- Work the program for 30 minutes and be prepared to tell me 10 new ideas generated.

Flash cards

- Make flash cards using the vocabulary terms on the board. Learn them.
- Make flash cards using any 15 key terms from the chapter. Learn them.

Bulletin board construction

- With a partner, design and display a bulletin board showing (the process of photosynthesis).

Posters

- On poster board, make a full color poster showing (the taxonomic divisions in the plant Kingdom).

Dioramas

- Construct a diorama for any scene in the book.
- Working with 3 classmates, each construct a diorama depicting (a different major biome). Be prepared to discuss differences.

Constructing books/booklets

- Make a booklet persuading (a vote for water fluoridation).
- Design a booklet as (Samuel Adams may have for the colonists to incite a revolution).
- Design and illustrate a children's book on(how to prevent disease).

Collagés

- Make a collage using 3 different mediums showing (smoking propaganda).
- Work with a partner to make a collage (debating the draft). Each person take an opposing side.

Mobiles

- Make a mobile of (the Order Hymenoptera).

Models

- Build an edible model of (a cell).
- Build a model of (an amniotic egg) using material other than paper.

Board games

- Construct a board game teaching (cell division). The game must teach all stages. Have 2 classmates play the game.

"Pay no attention to the man behind the curtain."

- The wizard of Oz

Chapter Four

The Middle Layer: The "B" level

The purpose of the middle layer is to have students apply information learned in the bottom layer. This "B" layer is designed to require a higher level of thinking than the "C" layer. The layer is called the "B" level because students wanting a grade of a "B" are going to have to work into this layer.

In my design, I included traditional rote memorization and drill types of learning into the bottom layer. I wanted each layer to require more thinking than the previous level. So the "B" level asks students to **apply, discover, hypothesize, or problem solve**. The layer must remain smaller than the "C" level because in order to cover most states' core curriculum mandates, students need to get the bulk of their points in the lower level.

As a science teacher designing Layered Curriculum, I could easily see that the "B" layer was the place to put problem solving laboratory activities. But I wanted true problem solving, as opposed to traditional lab work out of a lab manual. A *lab-manual* type lab, while proclaiming problem solving, really is not. It generally provides a thorough list of materials needed. It also includes a step-by-step procedure and a proper format for presenting data. After measuring, mixing and doing "something" according to the written instructions, students might answer some questions posed at the end which asked for reflection on what they've done.

This is not problem solving. This requires little original thinking on the part of the student. I want students to really think and problem solve here. So, for the "B" level, I simply pose several questions. These are written in the middle layer on the unit sheet. The questions involve materials readily available in the classroom or community. The students choose one question to answer. It is important to only provide the question. I do not help with their procedure or solution. I will help them gather needed materials, but they must tell me what those materials are.

Here are some examples of "B" level questions I've used in my general biology class:

- How fast does a worm move in m.p.h.?
- What percent of a plant is water?
- How much weight can a snail pull?
- Does water temperature affect plant growth?
- Which holds more water proportionately, a paper towel or a natural sponge?
- Who jumps further proportionately, you or a cricket?
- Does Scope really kill bacteria?
- Do Rolaids reduce acid levels?

In the beginning, students will naturally ask for help, with questions like "How do I do the one with the snail?"

My response is "I have no idea, that's your problem to solve."

In the beginning this creates a great deal of frustration on the part of the student.

Expect responses like "You're the teacher, you're supposed to help us," or "If you don't know, how are we supposed to figure it out."

My response continues to be "I won't help you with ideas, but I'll be happy to help you with materials when you decide what you need."

You know you are succeeding when you hear students proclaim "Well, don't ask her, she won't help." It may take several attempts before the students will give up on you for procedures and have to resort to using their own brains for problem solving.

Again, they may realize school is for the students, not the teacher.

Another point here is that I frequently ask questions that I do not know the answer to myself. I simply sit around on the week-ends and think up fun questions that a 16 year old might like to play around with. The great part about not knowing the answer myself comes at the end. When students finish a lab, they always want to know "Is that the *right* answer?" I can reply, "I don't know, I was asking you!" It always takes them by surprise. But, the student is finding out that real problem solving doesn't always have a *right* answer and that teachers may not always have the answers either. Sometimes we enjoy learning right along with the students.

Grading the "B" level

The "B" level assignments are worth 15 points. Grading these problem-solving activities is relatively easy. You can assess them in a number of ways. You may again use an oral defense to have students discuss their work with you. This works well with younger students, students who struggle with writing, or any population where an oral defense would be preferable. You can have the students write their work up in a formal presentation or make a display. For a problem solving lab, I like students to write five things:

1. What were they trying to find out? (question)
2. What did they think would happen? (hypothesis)
3. What did they do? (procedure)
4. What happened? (results)
5. Where they correct? (conclusion)

I also discuss their work with them, especially if they've worked in a group. Credit is given based on the logic they used in designing their procedure and their explanation. Their results must also be reasonable.

Reasonable is generally defined by me. For example, let's look at the problem of "how fast does a worm move in m.p.h.?" Suppose a student finishes and me that the worm moved 764 miles per hour. Well, I don't really know how fast a worm moves, but my guess is that it's not quite that fast, and we might want to go back and re-examine her procedure. But if the answer looks reasonable and they've managed a logical attempt at solving the problem, they've passed this assignment.

The purpose of this level is original application or discovery on the part of the student. Assessment is looking for that. Has the student done some original thinking? Have they processed information and then applied it in a creative manner? This level should demonstrate learning beyond the rote storage of facts which was done at the "C" level.

The "B" level doesn't have to involve a lab. Depending on your subject, look for ways in which the students can creatively apply information they learned in the "C" level. Have them design a geometric plan using new math concepts. Have them write stories using new vocabulary words. Have them apply concepts learned into a work setting. Each student product should be unique in that it is the product of their unique mind. For that reason it is difficult to grade based on the idea of right or wrong. Instead you are looking for a process.

This level should also be enticing. The activities themselves should draw students up from the "C" level. This prevents students from getting a "C" and stopping at that point. A common question I get from teachers is "what do you do with students who attain a "C", are happy with it, and quit there?" If that is the case, then the problem is with your "B" level. In working with adolescents I say, "think edible or gross". You want assignments out of the ordinary, something they can eat, something they must do outside, something requiring them to handle a disgusting cricket, etc. You want them to look forward to finishing the "C" level so that they can get to the "B" level.

Chapter Five

The Top Layer-- The "A" level

In my opinion, the ultimate goal of educators is to turn out students who can critically think about an issue in their lives long after I'm gone. Life calls upon us, sometimes daily, to make a **critical analysis** of an issue. Our old car breaks down and we have to decide whether to make an expensive repair or replace it. We are asked to vote on the person who can best represent us in government. A job opportunity arises and we must decide to take it or leave it. We give birth to a child with serious disabilities, how do we proceed in that child's best interest. These are the kinds of critical thinking tasks we must do in real life. And that is what I ask my students to do to a topic in order to get an "A".

I want students to analyze an issue, research the facts, and form an opinion. One of the most common complaints among educators at all levels, from kindergarten to college is that students can't or won't "think". What they are really complaining of is that students often lack critical thinking skills. Students must be taught the process of making a critical analysis. The purpose of the "A" level is to teach this process.

Here at this level, I again pose several questions. These are questions for which there is no necessarily agreed upon answer. Examples of questions I ask at this level are:

- What should be done with frozen embryos?
- When will we have a vaccine for AIDS?
- Is the chicken pox vaccine a good idea?
- Was there ever life on Mars?
- What really happened to the dinosaurs?
- Is there a flesh-eating bacteria?
- Should people with serious mental disabilities be allowed to marry and have children?

The point at the "A" level is to offer questions where students can find more than one side to the issue. The students working at this level choose one question from the list. The assignment requires library research. I provide a form for them to use, called the "A" level assignment sheet (see page 30). The form asks them to find and summarize three recent magazine or journal articles on the subject.

In addition to summarizing each article, the students must also cite them correctly. This is a challenge as many teacher know when they see a citation such as "the computer in the library". Citing articles correctly is especially difficult given this day of the Internet. Many of us are not always sure of how to cite a particular reference. We spend time at the beginning of the year learning how to cite things correctly.

After researching, reading and summarizing three articles, the student must form an opinion on the issue. This opinion is written on the back of the form in two good paragraphs (defined as 3-5 complete sentences each). Students are graded on grammar, punctuation and spelling on this assignment.

All students can learn this procedure. All students, regardless of ability or disability can critically think. Even a 16 year old with serious mental disabilities can easily answer such questions as, "Which is better, Nintendo 64 or Sony Play Station?" Not only will they give you their opinion, they can critically defend it!

And where did they get their information? Probably from a variety of sources, friends, television, ads, etc. They've taken these sources' opinions, bounced them around a little in their own mind and come up with an opinion. This is a critical analysis. Students simply need to be shown the procedure.

Grading "A" level assignments

These "A" level assignments are worth 20 points. Students receive up to 5 points for each summarized article (2 points for a correct citation and 3 points for summary) and 5 points for their opinion. In order to get credit, they must form an opinion one way or the other on the issue. It doesn't matter what their opinion is or even whether or not it matches the research, but they do need to take a stand on the issue.

Occasionally I'll have students in my class who have a writing disability. Writing is so slow or painfully difficult for them, that filling out the "A" level assignment sheet would be an overwhelming tasks. In addition, I frequently have students who are extremely poor readers. For these students I make the additional accommodation that the "A" level may be done orally. So, even if a parent or resource teacher helps them find the information and even reads the articles to them, that student must come in during class or even after school and give me their oral report. The must explain or summarize the three articles and give me their opinion or critical analysis on the topic.

"A" level assignment Sheet.   20   points

Name_____

Unit #_____   Topic #____   Period:_____

Summarize 3 recent magazine or journal articles on your topic. On the back of this sheet write 2 good paragraphs (5 -7 sentences make a good paragraph) on your opinion. Make sure to mention some of the research in your opinion.

1.Title of Article:
Title of Magazine or Journal:
Author:
Date of Article:
Summary:

2.Title of Article:
Title of Magazine or Journal:
Author:
Date of Article:
Summary:

3.Title of Article:
Title of Magazine or Journal:
Author:
Date of Article:
Summary:

Chapter Six

Adapting Layered Curriculum for Other Subjects and Grade Levels

Many teachers, because of their grade level, subject matter, or teaching style do not feel comfortable offering Layered Curriculum in a completely open and optional manner. Often times, certain material must be presented in a sequential manner or is best presented in a whole class method. In addition, many teachers are faced with liability issues, illiteracy, and school policy. Fortunately, the creative minds of teachers can work thorough nearly any obstacle.

Modifying for English Novels

If you are teaching the novel *Huck Finn*, it is difficult to leave reading the book as an optional assignment. For this reason, most teachers who successfully use Layered Curriculum have some parts of the unit required. Generally the first couple of assignments are required of all students. So, if you are teaching a unit on *Huck Finn*, you might require:

#1. Read the book.
#2. Participate in class discussion.
#3. Do one character analysis.

The student can then choose from the remainder of the assignments to finish off their grade.

I know of some English teachers who have managed to work through the *reading* part of novel assignments by offering a choice in reading. They recognize that some students struggle with reading and the novel would take much longer to get through, and that many students prefer silent individual reading. In their classes, they offer the option of both.

The teacher reads the novel, once, into a tape. Students may sit at a listening center, using headphones and follow along in their novels, or they may use the time for silent individual reading. Either way, the novel is read and time is easier to plan. This is especially effective if you have a wide diversity of reading levels and abilities in your class.

Modifying for Honors and Advanced Placement Classes

In my Advanced Placement class, I use a slightly different model. In AP Biology, the curriculum is long, difficult, and we are teaching to a very specific national exam at the end. There is a tremendous amount of material which we have to get through. Even more of a factor, my AP classes are not quite so diverse a group of learners, and do not require so many assignment choices. Therefore, the entire "C" level is required of my students and presented as *whole-class* instruction.

When I say *whole-class instruction* I mean that I do not present the "C" level as such, on paper. The assignments that I would normally put in the "C" level are simply class policy. So the class requirements are that students attend class, take lecture notes, read the chapters, and do a certain number of textbook review questions. Meeting these minimum requirements, however, will only get the student a grade of "C".

If you know AP students, a "C" grade is simply not an option in their world. So I then present to them a small, half sheet unit which gives them a choice of research, lab, and critical thinking questions which they can then choose from to finish off their grade. I even separate the assignments into "B" and "A" level activities. The structure is similar to what I use in my general class. The "B" level consists of problem solving lab activities which they do on their own or in pairs and "A" level assignments which require library research and a critical analysis.

I also use oral assessment for the class activities in AP classes because of the importance I feel in helping students connect class and homework activities and learning.

In addition to our class activities, labs and research, we have a formal written exam at the end of each unit which counts for half their unit grade. So a 100 point unit will come with a 100 point exam. The exams are traditional exams designed to mimic the types of questions found on AP tests. I include free response questions which the students read and grade themselves from a written criteria. Again, this is designed to mimic the AP testing situation.

Modifying for Liability Issues

What do you do if your subject includes things like power saws, Bunsen burners, open flame, chemical hazards and the like? Obviously the thought of letting students work independently while you are doing oral assessment across the room, probably terrifies you. It would me. Teachers with these issues have solved the problem by offering these assignment choices on certain days.

For example, in one chemistry class, all labs are done on the third day of the unit.

The teacher informs the students that "All labs will be done on day three. If you are planning to do a lab on this unit, plan it for day three. I will not be correcting any other assignments on that day as I will be spending my time supervising the lab area."

You may need to offer lab days, cooking days, construction days, etc. more or less often depending on your subject. You may want to have entire class periods for lecture and some days with no direct instruction whatsoever. These days would be for student work or labs.

Modifying for Traditional Versus Block Schedule

One of the things I've learned from traveling throughout the country and visiting schools is that every district has a different definition for **block scheduling.** I would start talking to teachers about teaching on a block and halfway through the conversation would realize that we were talking about different things.

The school where I currently teach runs on an odd-even block schedule. This means that we meet our students every other day for an 80 minute period. Students attend their odd (1, 3, 5, 7) period classes one day and their even (2, 4, 6, 8) period classes the next. There are many versions of this expanded class schedule across the country. Some schools meet everyday for 80 minutes but the class lasts only half the year. This creates problems with Advanced Placement classes as the course sometimes ends far from the exam. Some schools meet odd-even blocks on Monday through Thursday with all classes meeting on Friday for a short 40 minute period. Some schools mix block classes meeting every other day with some shorter classes which meet every day. The variation is enormous.

Of course, there is even variation in the **traditional school schedule**. Some schools run on 6 periods, some 7 and some even try for 8. And I've seen schools that rotate the classes so each day starts with a different period. (This is an idea whose theory I love, but never having taught it, I think I'd go crazy). Then, there's all those divided lunch period options, but let's not even go into that. So your class periods can be 40 to 80 minutes, depending on the school.

I have had the opportunity to teach on only two of these types of schedules, the odd-even block which I'm currently on and the traditional six period day. I've used Layered Curriculum on both schedules and it works fine, although differently.

On the block, I have time to lecture briefly, every day, allow five minutes for planning and getting materials, and get around to every student at least twice before the five minute clean-up. It is the schedule I prefer.

However, I was also able to work with the traditional daily periods. Here I would only lecture every other day so that we had some days where the entire period was spent on individual student work and assessment. I could still get around to every student at least one time before the five minute clean-up. Students were only allowed library time on the days where there was no lecture. I found that students who went to the library after the lecture, did not have enough time in the library to make it worth their leaving the room. Certain days were designated as lab days.

Depending on how often and how long you meet your students, you may have to modify Layered Curriculum. But I've never seen a schedule that it can't work in. If you have long and short days mixed, you may try saving the short days for testing, lecture, and quizzes and keep the longer periods for student work, labs and research.

Modifying for Lower Elementary Grades

Teachers have found all types of creative solutions for using Layered Curriculum and *keeping score* with younger children. The *learning centers* design is the most familiar solution for creating a classroom for non-readers.

Use color-coded tokens, popsicle sticks, cards, etc. to help students keep track of objectives mastered and areas visited. All assignments designed to teach a specific objective would offer the same color token. Students need to collect tokens of various colors and the teacher can set policy as to how many and which color.

Modifying for College and Adult Learners

Layered Curriculum is particulary useful in teaching adult learners. Adults, like children, are most creative when empowered with a sense of control. I have used a modified version of Layered Curriculum in several college classes that I've taught. It especially helps with the problems encountered in one night a week or all-day Saturday type classes.

Adults are a special student population in that they have other significant community responsibilities outside of the classroom (worker, boss, mother, father, spouse). Instructors must be especially mindful of the variety of ways in which these adults have included school into their lives. Many adults have extra time between classes to devote to the course, and many have very limited time outside the scheduled class time.

I also found that many adult learners are fatigued during long class periods and may not work best during a long three to five hour session.

You may start to see the possibilities that Layered Curriculum allows for in adult classrooms. Lectures may be optional and worth a certain number of points. Obviously most learners will attend the lectures as the material presented is important, interesting and beneficial. However, occasionally the student may have to miss class or come late due to some other unforseen obligation. This allows the student the option to make up those points with alternative assignments.

The same holds true with non-lecture activities such as group discussions, videos, and other activities held inside the classroom. The students can choose to stay and participate in the activities or if they have to leave early, or are simply too tired to fully participate one evening, other options are available for them with between-class activities.

Outside research projects are more productive when students feel they have a choice in the topic. Here you may want to offer three or four topic choices for the student. Instructors may also offer optional forms for research presentations - written report, display, or oral presentation.

In my classes, I wrote up a unit of assignment options for each unit. It consisted of attending the lecture, films, outside investigations, journal research, projects from the textbook, groups discussions, video, etc. In the three hour course, my lecture and class discussion took the bulk of the time. However, the last part of the class involved one of the other activities. Students could stay and participate in the video, discussion, project, etc. or leave and do one of the outside projects during the week. This worked very well in my class population. Students enjoyed having that choice and felt that the class really accommodated the needs of the adult learner. Some students had only that particular block of time allocated from work, children, and other responsibilities and stayed the whole class time to participate. However some, too tired that late in the evening, attended the lecture and discussion, but left early for home knowing they would have an activity to complete on own during the week.

Chapter Seven

Tips, Hints and Suggestions

I have been using Layered Curriculum in my own classroom for about five years now. In addition, I have worked with thousands of teachers in modifying Layered Curriculum for a variety of subjects and settings. Here are some of the logistical strategies we've found to work best.

Tips:

Color code the unit sheets. My classes do four units per quarter, eight per semester, 16 per year. Each is copied on a different color. It's much easier to just refer to the "green unit" or the "red unit". At the end of a grading quarter, they can quickly pull out their "yellow, green, red and blue" sheets, add them up, and they have their grade. This helps all of us stay organized.

Worried about students losing their unit sheet? On the first day of school, **give every student a file folder**. Have a file cabinet in the room with a drawer for each period. Allow students to leave their materials in the room if they need to.

Keep a bucket of extra pencils and pens. I pick up spares in the halls or on my floor and throw them in the bucket. We all want students to come prepared, but some students struggle with the simplest of organizational skills and we can help them most by not making a big deal out of it.

Check out the policies of your local Public Broadcasting television station for using taped programs in your classroom. Most have policies giving schools re-broadcast rights for at least a year. Some of the educational daily programs make excellent video options for units. You may find that some of the programing has a teacher guide available.

The daily newspaper can be brought in each day. Many cities offer the newspaper for free to teachers and schools (paid for by vacation newspapers in the community). Let students find articles pertaining to the unit.

Display and hang as much student work as possible. When students know that their work is going to be displayed, they invest more effort. Also investigate hanging or displaying some in the hall outside your room. Although most elementary schools fill the hall with student work, this tradition gets lost in secondary schools.

Post grading rubrics everywhere(see chapter 12). It may help to color code the rubrics as well. Then when a student asks about how to do an assignment, you can just refer him to the pink sheet on the back wall.

Hints:

As students finish "C" level assignments, **sign them off right on their unit sheets**. I simply initial the assignment and put the point value next to it. If you'd like a back-up, you may also put the points earned on the actual assignment before putting it away. This helps if there is a dispute, or a student has to reassemble her unit sheet because the "dog ate it."

Putting the points in the margins of the unit sheet will also give students a visual reminder of what they've done. If you put a grading scale and due date on the units as well, students get a visual of
1. How far they've come.
2. Where they want to go.
3. When they need to be there.

When starting this teaching methodology, **go slow.** Design and try one unit and see how it goes. Keep notes and modify for the next unit. The first one is the hardest. One you have a workable plan, it's just a matter of cut and paste on your word processor.

Also remember to **go with your comfort level.** If your teaching style does not allow as much student choice as mine, then don't offer so much. Layered Curriculum can be done in dozens of modified ways. Perhaps you are more comfortable giving whole class instruction for the entire "C" level. If so, then maybe you could allow some student choice in the application and critical thinking levels.

If you have students who are proficient in a foreign language, have them **translate a couple of unit sheets into their native language**. This makes a good resource if you have new students transfer in who read little or no English. It is nice to have something in their own language to get them started. It won't be the same unit everyone else is working on, but at least you have something to get them engaged with. Assignments on this would have to be done with illustrations or some other non-language based form.

Use the last 5 minutes for clean-up. I sometimes offer job choices for an extra five points per unit. Students can sign up to do a clean-up job each of the days for a particular unit. Jobs might include: organizing textbooks, organizing art supplies, clean up t.v. area, shut down computers, trash, making sure desks and chairs are put back. When everyone leaves and the dust settles, you can easily see who has done their job. This is especially helpful if you teach a wide variety of subjects and have to start fresh with the next class.

Suggestions

For Visual Learners

Supplement your lectures with visuals. In addition to just notes on the board or transparencies, try to use models, charts and other visual aides. Even when offering a taped lecture or reading, set out visual props for students to look at or manipulate during their listening time.

Provide all students with a **written copy** of assignments.

Whenever possible, **write a backup** on the board for any verbal instruction or direction.

Allow **written reports** as an alternative to oral ones.

Provide a **written copy of board work** for those who may need it. For example, if the vocabulary words are written on the board, it may be helpful to some to have a few photocopies of the words made. Many students get lost/distracted in copying from the board to the paper and back again.

When discussing abstract concepts use **visual representations** or allow students to use or make manipulative objects.

Use visuals like bulletin boards, posters, transparencies and graphs. However, be careful with a visually busy classroom. Some students are overwhelmed and distracted with too much visual information. You may want to a have a visually quiet area of the room as well.

In addition to textbooks, have students **read other things** such as newspapers, bulletin boards, maps, magazines, brochures, or labels.

For Auditory Learners

Record assignment directions on tape so students can access them as needed. Some students have extremely poor reading skills, so although they can sound the words out in reading the assignment, they have no comprehension. It helps if you take the first day of a unit and read the entire thing out loud.

I've also found that I get a lot of "takers" if I **offer to read magazine articles**. Magazine articles are a favorite assignment choice of my students, but many struggle with reading. So I may say, "I'm going to read the Chicken Pox article aloud in that back corner. If anyone would like to come and listen, they are welcome." I'm amazed at the turn-out.

Have a variety of textbooks available for different reading levels. Textbook salespeople are a great resource for this. When they ask if they can send you a sample copy of a particular book, always accept. You can get a huge assortment of reading material this way. Also, be sure to inquire as to whether or not a Spanish audio version of a textbook is available. More and more publishers are offering it.

Tape record certain textbook chapters. You can sit in the comfort and quiet of your home on a Sunday afternoon, and read a chapter into a tape recorder. You may want to simplify the vocabulary when possible. The assignment is for the students to read along while listening to you read through headphones. At the end they can come to you and have their oral defense. When I tried this I was so very surprised at how many students choose the assignment. I now offer it frequently.

Give oral and written quizzes. Offer them as options. Some students like reading quizzes straight from the publisher printed copy.

Offer a **variety** of ways for students to verbalize ideas. Try class presentations, small group presentation, oral reports, discussion groups, debates, and panels.

For Tactile Learners

Have manipulative objects for abstract ideas. Better yet, have students build the manipulative objects themselves.

Keep a table of art and craft supplies in the room. Include string, scissors, playdoh, construction paper, markers, baggies, etc. Allow students to use a variety of materials in creating models.

Have students measure properties such as temperature, weight, size and distance. This is especially fun if the object is very large. Also, have them make scaled drawings or representations of large objects.

Dioramas are still fun, no matter what grade you teach. Remember, they are those displays, models and representations put in a shoe box or other small box.

Mobiles, out a various materials, are simple and great options for tactile learners.

Have students construct a board game teaching a certain number of concepts. To pass it off, they must play it in a group.

Drawings, charts and graphs are excellent activities. You may occasionally want them presented on something other than on plain paper. Try 3-D graphs or having them display them on a bulletin board.

Have students build models, maps, bulletin boards.

Chapter Eight

The Biology of Layered Curriculum

The last two or three decades have brought an abundance of new research on brain function and learning styles. Neuropsychology and educators are still digging through all the results trying to make sense out of it all and understanding how best to apply it in the classroom. However, some of the main ideas that continue to come from the research are easily implemented in our classrooms. Some of this research supports what we already know and some is shedding new light on old problems.

The Issue of *Choice*

There are many parts to students' brains. But the two most critical to the classroom are the cortex and the hypothalamus. The cortex is the top layer of the brain. It is the squiggly mass you see when you look at the brain and the part most of us think of when we think of a brain. It is actually a very thin layer of tissue, just six layers thick which wraps and covers the more primitive layers underneath.

The cortex houses most of our learning. This is where you store all your algebra, history, English, physics, knitting instruction, Barney songs, etc. Everything you "learn" is stored, for the most part, in the cortex. As classroom teachers, this is the part we are trying to reach. Unfortunately, due to the way the brain works, we have to get through the more primitive layers in order to reach the cortex. It would be handy for educators if the brain's priorities were top-down, but fortunately for our survival, the priority is bottom-up. Let me clarify.

As I mentioned, the parts underneath the cortex are more primitive. By that I mean we share those underneath parts with more primitive animals, they develop first and they "fire" or react first. These areas are basically responsible for our physical survival. They keep us alive in this world by running our bodies, regulating body activity, and reacting to life-threatening events in our environment. If there's time left-over, we can involve our cortex. So, in order to reach the cortex to store information on Civil War battles, we must make sure that the remainder of the brain is assured of basic survival.

One of the key players in survival, is a small area of the brain called the **hypothalamus**. Lying underneath the cortex, the hypothalamus controls a great deal of primitive needs. It is in charge of the primitive emotions - anger, aggression and fear. It also controls the fight or flight response, hunger, thirst, the sex drive, body temperature, water balance and the endocrine system of hormones. That's a lot of responsibility for a small region of the brain.

Apparently you are born with the hypothalamus up and running and ready for survival. It is the most primitive area of the brain that controls behavior. It generally reacts first in any situation perceived as threatening. Most of us are familiar with the sudden engagement of our hypothalamus (just think of the last time an event made you angry). While the hypothalamus is engaged, the rational thinking logic of the cortex is basically ignored as the "survival-at-all-costs" logic of the hypothalamus is in charge (just think of the last time an event made you angry). Often times the behaviors exhibited by an individual during "hypothalamus engagement" may not be judged as behaviors best suited in the long-run (just think of the last time an event made you angry).

Perhaps you see now, how teaching is difficult when surrounded by a group of students with their *hypothalamus engaged*. Some students (and adults) spend an awful lot of time using this part of their brain. They are called hypothalamus-driven individuals. I'm sure you know many of them (they seem to accumulate in 7th period). What causes this type of personality? A variety of factors enter into the display of primitive emotions, but one of the main reasons has to do with the basic biology of the brain.

The brain is nothing more than a mass of nerve cells, called neurons, held together with some glial cells. Whenever you think a thought, you are basically just firing a pathway of neurons through your brain with electricity and chemicals. The more often you fire a pathway, the easier it gets to fire. So the more often you look at someone's face, the easier it is to recognize. The more often you hear a tune, the easier it is to sing along, and so on.

This works in all parts of the brain. So those people who live in "fight or flight" worlds spend a lot of time firing pathways in the hypothalamus. The more it's fired, the easier it is to fire and the more likely it is to fire. So if you have students whose home and family life revolves basically around eat-or-be-eaten, they are likely to be hypothalamus-driven individuals. Their brains easily fall into survival mode and their behaviors reflect that.

So, what's a teacher to do? It boils down to one simple word. Control. People want **control**. It is a basic need for survival. All of us want control, because that is the what satisfies the hypothalamus and allows us to use other parts of our brain, mainly the cortex. Satisfying the survival needs of the hypothalamus should be the first priority of a classroom teacher. If the hypothalamus isn't content, the cortex will not respond to teaching. The first thing which needs to be done is to establish an environment of trust, safety and the perception of control. If we are in control, our survival is not threatened, we are free to learn, create and grow.

The easiest way to allow students to feel control in the classroom is through choice. When students get to make choices in a classroom, they feel in control. When they feel in control, they take ownership in the activity and the behaviors exhibited are rational, logical behaviors determined by the cortex as opposed to the hypothalamus. When teachers allow students that type of control, the entire dynamic of the class changes. The us-verus-them mentality disappears, teachers are seen by students more as a coach on their side, learning is facilitated, and teaching is fun.

As much as possible, allow choice. You may not be able to allow total and complete choice on everything, but that shouldn't be the case anyway. The teacher must have some control as well. The teacher controls the curriculum and the direction of the course. But generally, within guidelines, there are places to allow students control as well. It may just be a choice in the order in which they do something. It may just be a choice in the way an assignment is presented or maybe just a choice in assessment or homework. But any time you can allow choice, you increase the student's perception of control and you decrease the likelihood of disruptive, non-productive behaviors stemming from the hypothalamus.

Choice should be given not just in assignments, but in social needs and physical structure in the classroom. The original learning styles research showed us how some children wanted to work with their friends. Others wanted to work in a pair, a group, or alone. Some worked best with the teacher no where in sight, while others would write one word, check to see if it was correct before writing their next word.

Examine ways in which the physical structure of your classroom can accommodate the various social needs of students. Allow a variety of seating choices. You may also allow a variety of teacher intervention strategies.

Circadian Rhythms

Another biological issue to consider is the time-of-day needs of students. Psychologists have known for years about circadian rhythm differences in humans. There are basically two groups of human circadian rhythms. One of the ways to determine your group is to look at body temperature changes throughout the day. For all of us, our body temperature is at its lowest point first thing in the morning, before we even get out of bed. In one group, that temperature stays relatively low until around 9:00 am when it starts to rise. It will stay elevated until about 10:00 or 11:00 at night. These people are called *larks*.

In the second group, the body temperature stays low in the morning until around noon, then rises and stays high until somewhere between midnight and 2:00 a.m.. These people are called *owls*. Most of us know which group we are in. For the most part, pre and post adolescents are larks and adolescents are owls. The average person is born into the world as a lark. In their early childhood they enjoy getting up early (early morning cartoons took advantage of this) and getting to bed by 9:00 pm was no problem. Somewhere around the age of 10,11, or 12, most people magically turn into owls. They no longer enjoy seeing the sun come up. Noon seems are more reasonable hour to rise and staying out until the wee hours of the morning is not a problem. This clock runs usually until the early to mid 20's when once again we change back into a lark. There are all kinds of exceptions to this as many of us post-adolescent owls know.

Traditionally we have blamed these changes on social events such as leaving college and getting out into the real world. It has nothing to do with joining the real world, but more on the fact that leaving college coincided with the age of 24 or 25 when most owls change back into a lark.

Although all this information was made available a couple of decades ago, education is still lagging behind the research in practical application. This can be seen in the starting times of most junior and senior high schools. Although we know the majority of our students at this age are *owls* we start most schools at 7:30 or 8:00 in the morning.

Obviously we are not running the schools for the students, but rather for the teachers, administrators and other adults. I have often heard people say that students could function at this early hour if they really wanted to and should just "try harder." Trying harder is not the issue. The problem lies in the basic biology of the adolescent. They really function better later in the day.

Besides creating time-of-day learning issues, the start time of schools also brings up another issue of concern to school boards in recent years. School boards have been debating the critical time period between 3:00 and 5:00 p.m. known as the *pregnancy hour*. Apparently most teen risk-taking activity occurs during these afternoon hours. That's the time teens become pregnant, engage in drug experimentation and criminal activity. It is the time between when school is dismissed and most parental supervision resumes.

It seems obvious to many that simply pushing back the school day at the secondary level would begin to address these two significant issues. A few districts in recent years are beginning to push the starting times back, but not far enough. Most districts opt to try 30 or 60 minutes later so that the day begins at 8:30-ish, but they should really be looking at starting at 10:00 or later. Of course this would create new problems for teachers who are primarily larks and prefer the early hours.

Why aren't more schools looking at later start times? The most common reason given is that a later start time would interfere with athletic activities after school. Bureaucratic tradition is often the bane of creative problem solving.

Light

Another issue addressed by researchers but not educators is the differing needs of students for light. The light issue has shown new problems since the advent of the windowless classroom schools which were popular in the 1970's and 80's. For reasons I have never fully understood, architects during that 20 year period felt classrooms would be better without the distractions provided by windows (as though there were no distractions inside the classroom). Unfortunately many teachers today are stuck with these classrooms which creates emotional problems in both students and teachers, especially in the winter.

People need light, particularly natural light, for a certain period each day in order to have a normal secretion of the chemical melatonin. Melatonin is used to regulate sleep cycles and other chemicals for normal emotional stability. People who do not have enough light exposure can get depressed and have sleep problems. Depression in some young people leads to problems with aggression and impulsive behavior. Fluorescent light does not give off the right color waves to produce melatonin. So in the winter children often come to school in the dark, sit under fluorescent light all day, get out in the afternoon (often under cloudy, gray skies) then head straight home and inside for the remainder of the day. Often there is not enough opportunity for the light exposure needed for normal production of melatonin.

About the only thing a teacher can do if stuck in a windowless classroom is to try to supplement light with incandescent light bulbs (the screw-in lightbulb kind we use in our homes). The higher wattage, the better. This will help provide some of the light you and your students need.

Chapter Nine

Frequently Asked Questions

F ollowing are the most frequently asked questions from my website, newsletters and workshops.

Do Students have to start with the "C" level, then do the "B", then "A"?

Not always. Students can start anywhere on the unit sheet. Many students prefer to start with the "A" or "B" level assignments and then finish up with bottom layer material.

When I first started using this style of instruction, I insisted that students start at the bottom and work up. But, I discovered that for many of my reluctant learners, the "B" level was the place to engage them.

All teachers are familiar with the reluctant learner - that's the student who walks in on day one and puts his head down on the desk. They've had so many years of failure that the learned helplessness has set in and they don't even try. This is the student that I can frequently engage by putting a snail down on his desk and asking him how much weight he thinks that snail can pull. Then ask him to prove it.

Nearly any student would rather play with a snail than lay with his head on the desk. All children would rather do something than nothing. The problem of doing nothing in class generally stems from a lack of interest and a perceived lack of control.

If you observe students out in the community, rarely do you see a child doing nothing. Look in a mall, or a museum, or at a park. Children are active. They are naturally inquisitive and when left with choices will explore, learn and discover. We need to allow this same natural tendency to work in the classroom as well.

Of course, if student's start in the "B" or "A" level, remind them that that doesn't give them a "B" or "A". They will still need to fill out the remainder of their points from the bottom, "C" level.

Ideally, a unit should build through the layers. Basic content in the "C" layer, application in the "B" layer of concepts learned below, and then a critique in the "A" layer. This is the goal, however from a practical standpoint, it may be better to let them work through the layers in random order.

Can Students do more than one "B" or "A" level assignment?

In my classes, no. I have many students ask this same question. They just want to do three library critical thinking questions and be finished. I've set Layered Curriculum up as a triangle shaped learning model. The bottom layer is the widest, because that is the area where students build their foundation in general knowledge. If they only did "B" or "A" level assignments, they would miss out on the opportunity to collect that general level knowledge.

From a practical point, my students, like many across the country, are required to take an end-of-the-year exam given by the state. I am held accountable for teaching the minimum state core requirements. I can't do this, if students only work the middle and top layers.

Do you lecture?

Yes, I lecture everyday. However, they are all offered as an option.

At the beginning of class, I put an outline on the overhead while students are coming in and settling down. I tell the students, "This is the topic I'll be covering today in lecture. If you are going to listen and take notes, copy down the outline. If you are not doing that assignment please find something quiet to do for the next 10 minutes. "

I spend about 10 to 15 minutes lecturing. Student can listen and takes notes, or quietly work on some other activity. Notes are worth 5 points a day. Surprisingly, almost all my students choose this assignment. They quietly listen and take their notes from the outline.

I say surprisingly because we have all seen what happens when we require students to do notes. If I said to my class, "today we will all take notes. Get out paper and pencil, put away all your other materials, listen to me and write down things I say".

Suddenly about half of them would need a nap and the other half would remember that they needed to reorganize their purses. It's amazing what happens when you give students choice. As mentioned in an earlier chapter, giving choice puts students in control. They choose whether or not to listen. Because it's their choice, not mine, they take ownership and interest.

I tell them they can listen or not listen, it makes no difference to me. Of course, they all learn that I cover a great deal of information in those lectures which they will need in order to complete other assignments on the unit sheet. If they choose not to listen, however they do need to work quietly on other tasks without disturbing us.

They also must be present to get credit for notes, so this helps reduce problems with being tardy. If they are absent or late, they are welcome to copy notes from a classmate so that they will have the information for their other assignments, but they do not get the credit of the lecture notes.

Does your course follow a textbook?

I try not to have any course I teach center around a textbook. I like students to view textbooks as a resource - one of several places to gather information. So for that reason, I do not have a class set of any particular book. I use several textbooks. I may have 10 or 15 different ones to choose from. I try to have an assortment for different reading levels. I have college level texts, high school, even elementary level textbooks. Students can find a book at their reading level.

I will issue students a textbook if they'd like one. They may choose any one in the room to check out. This really keeps the focus off of a textbook-driven curriculum. If there is a book assignment it may be done out of any of the books. The assignment might read "Find and read the chapter on Plant Reproduction from a textbook. Be prepared to answer the end of the chapter questions."

The assignments out of the lower level texts would not have the point value associated with them that the higher level textbooks do. This is especially true if there are specific book assignments or publisher generated worksheets which go with a specific book. Students could do several at a lower reading level to equal the tougher assignments at the higher level.

The same variety issue holds true with magazines and periodicals. I use a variety such as *Scientific American, USA Today, National Geographic*, even *Ranger Rick*. There is something for every reading ability.

How is your classroom set up?

My room is basically set up in resource and material centers. There are lab tables and other student desks in the middle. I have a small TV/VCR unit set up in one corner, a couple of computers in another area. Magazines and newspapers are set on a table in the front. In the back is our art supply area. This area has paper, glue, scissors, old texts and magazines to cut from, markers, crayons and string. A large bookcase houses most of the textbooks. An overhead projector is at the front.

Students do not need to work in a specific area (except for the videos and computer work). They can get their materials and come back to a table to work. I allow a five minute period between lecture notes and work time so that students can get their materials, books, video, etc. and get started.

With so much going on at one time, how do you monitor for destructive behavior?

This is a great question. My class is extremely student-centered. That means that students take responsibility for their learning. They have control over the assignments, pace and direction. Once control is shifted in a classroom from teacher to student, it is amazing how behaviors change as well.

Many years ago, I worked at a zoo in Oklahoma. One of my jobs was to tour elementary school students through the zoo when they came for field trips. Frequently, while touring the Pachyderm building on days when the elephants were indoors, we would experience a rather embarrassing situation. The elephants would pick up their own dung with their trunks, wait for the building to fill with children, and then hurl the dung at the students.

This behavior was hard to explain because it does not occur

(from what anyone can tell) in the wild. Zoo people call it "captive behavior". Other behaviors that fit into this category were the behaviors in the primate building where you would see the gorillas and other primates eating what you and I would consider quite disgusting material from the cage floor, or birds who were bald because they pulled out all their feathers. Anytime zoo people see behaviors in animals in zoos that are not seen in the wild, the catch-all phrase of "captive behavior" was used.

I include this story, because I firmly believe that much of what we teachers see in the school classroom is "captive behavior." Destructive and disruptive behaviors frequently occur when students feel captive and in situations with little or no control. Once students are given control, these behaviors tend to disappear.

Students want to learn and be creative, if given a situation in which they feel creative. When the teacher mandates assignments such as, "we're all going to read the chapter on Abraham Lincoln today" the student who doesn't enjoy learning through reading, or is a poor reader, may find his or her own way of being creative with the chapter on Abraham Lincoln. Those are the situations that cause Abe to have his teeth blacken out, or creative additions to the story inserted by students. Give students a choice, and not only are they not destructive, they are in fact, quite protective of, proud and invested in their assignment. Nearly all students are engaged in some task all the time. This too, reduces those "captive behaviors".

I won't tell you that all behavior problems completely disappear and you will never have another frustrating moment. There are no magic wands. However, a student-centered approach will greatly reduce your behavior problems. Some do continue to crop up and then you have to resort to your basic teacher skills to deal with them one-on-one.

In my classes, if I'm having a problem with a particular student, I generally choose a textbook assignment for him or her, take the student and the book work to another science class, and let them work in there for the day. (We have that arrangement in our department) At the end of that time, we discuss options and see if they'd like to return to class.

So most of your day is spent walking around your room?

Yes. Except for the 10 - 15 minutes of lecture, the rest of the period I walk around the room. I make sure everyone is working, help students find interesting and appropriate assignments, orally assess their "C" level assignments, and help organize materials. My school uses a block schedule so our periods are 80 minutes long. I can get around to all students at least twice each period, sometimes three times.

Even in my very large classes of 33-40 students, I can still get around to everyone twice. In a traditional 45 or 50 minute period, you would probably only get around once.

Do you have formal tests or other grades?

Not in my general biology classes. The unit sheets are the entire basis for grades. This gives complete control for both learning and grades to the student. I feel very strongly that the oral defense is a better assessment tool than my old paper and pencil tests I used years ago. I get a much better feel for what my students are learning and I can correct errors in thinking immediately. The students also understand that the oral assessment is a trade off for not having formal exams.

Layered Curriculum takes the mystery out of school and shifts the responsibility for learning from the teacher to the student, where it belongs. Students have complete control over their assignments and grades and are accountable for every class and homework assignment they do. On the first day of the term the students know how many points they need to accumulate during the term for the grade they want. Once students understand this concept, they love it - and parents too.

I can see how this works with science, but what about other disciplines?

Great question, and one of the most frequently asked. Layered Curriculum works in all subject areas and with all grade levels. I originally designed Layered Curriculum for my high school biology classes. I was not happy with the number of failures nor the level of student involvement and retention. After I'd worked out the method with my class, colleagues were asking how they might modify the method for their subjects. After some discussion, we found ways they could use this in their classes as well.

Soon the idea started spreading around the school and around my district. As teachers began making units, we could see a real need for a way to share the units with other teachers, so the help4teachers.com website went up. Originally a host for secondary lesson plans, the call started coming for elementary and college ideas as well, and so the website continued to evolve. Today the site hosts dozens of Layered Curriculum units sheets in grades from kindergarten to college and in nearly every subject you can think of. The creativity on the part of teachers is impressive.

English and Social Studies teachers have apparently found it extremely useful as the majority of the unit sheets we get come from those fields. However numerous examples are available in music, health, PE, math, art, foreign language, science, marketing, word processing. The list goes on and on.

Teachers use it for lower elementary, upper elementary and all the secondary subjects. Some sample unit sheets are found in chapter 16.

What do you do with students who finish early?

It doesn't happen too often as my units are structured so that it takes most students working all five days to complete the unit. One thing I do to help students pace themselves is I will not grade more than two "C" level assignments on any given day. This prevents them from saving them all up and bringing them in on day five. If they do that, they'll have to choose their favorite two assignments to be graded.

Once in awhile, I'll get a student who has completed the entire unit with a hour to spare. These are generally very bright students who don't create too many problems. I first give them the option of working on school work from another class. If they don't have something else to work on, I use them as aides and pre-graders. They may pre-grade or assist with flash card assignments or listen to magazine summaries. Sometimes I'll give them an article I'm going to use on the next unit and let them make a worksheet for it. Most students love to help in this way.

Under no circumstances are students allowed to just sit and do nothing in my room. I have a policy that my classroom is not a student lounge. If you are in the classroom, you must be doing something.

What do you do with a student who loses their unit sheet?

Believe it or not, it rarely happens. As I mentioned earlier, I keep a file cabinet in my room for student use. Each period has their own drawer. I encourage the students to keep their work, including their unit sheets in the room. However, there is a back-up plan.

As I discuss assignments with students I write the points received on the top of the assignment itself, as well as on the unit sheet. I keep all these assignments in a box. All the notes, bookwork, flash cards, worksheets, etc. go in the box. Art work such as mobiles, posters, and models are displayed. If a students should happen to lose his or her unit sheet sometime during the unit, they simply have to come in after school, pick up a new unit sheet and rummage through the box to find all their assignments so that we can put the unit back together. Generally, once this option is mentioned, they go home and find their lost unit sheet. I have had a few students who have actually lost their sheet and it's not that much of a problem for them. As I said, though, it is a rare occurrence.

Do some students still Fail?

Unfortunately, yes. It is still possible to fail, although you have to work at it really hard. Layered Curriculum was originally designed as a teaching method to reduce failures. And in that, it has succeeded. If students come to class and participate, they will generally pass. The biggest reason for failures is lack of attendance. I have some students, who for various reasons, come so sporadically that they simply cannot accumulate enough points.

I think what's important is to get students working. If a student is doing nothing, then the unit sheet is failing, not the students. Sometimes you have to visit individually with the child to find out what interests her and what type of assignment modification you may need to make to get her started. The key is to have something for everyone.

Can a student get a D?

Yes. Even though I refer to a "C", "B", and "A" level, it is possible to get a "D". On my grading scale, 40- 55 points on any unit is a "D". So if the student only accumulated points in that range, they'd have a "D" on the unit.

What about homework. Should it be optional?

Teachers have handled homework with Layered Curriculum in a numbers of ways. In my classes, homework would simply be part of the unit. If students work quickly and have an efficient use of their class time, then all work could be completed in class without homework. If they are slower, or absent, then some of the assignments may be done at home.

In fact, I always include activities that can be done from home. These would be things like finding and watching a documentary on television pertaining to the unit, looking for newspaper articles, and other sources of current events, or family field trips. Not only does this help involve parents in school work, it provides an option for students who are absent due to extended illness.

Some teachers have specific assigned activities that must be done as homework. These can either be included on the main unit sheet or given as a separate assignment. I know of a few schools, where only the homework is done as a Layered Curriculum unit. The class time is spent on whole-class instruction.

Again, this is an issue that can be modified to fit your individual needs or school requirements.

We could have saved you, but you cut us down, and soon you will be cut down and there'll be none of us to save you. - John Steinbeck.

Chapter Ten

Designing your Own Units

The first unit you design on your own will take you a long period of time. By "long period" I mean three or four hours on a Sunday afternoon. In all fairness, I must also warn you that your first unit may not be a total success. Most teachers tell me that their first unit was a mess, their second was almost workable, and by the third attempt they felt they got it.

The tricky part seems to be in getting the time and point system worked out. It is hard to judge how many assignments and how long to give students to work on the unit.

In designing your first unit, begin by choosing the amount of time you want to spend on the unit (i.e.: 5 days). Next, decide how many total points you want to give the unit (i.e.: 100 points). If you divide the total points by the number of days that will give you an idea of how many points per day students may work towards (100 points ÷ 5 = 20 points/day). This gives you a starting point. If you are going to give a brief lecture each day worth 5 points, that leaves 15 points for student work. If the work time is one hour, then a one hour assignment should be worth 15 points. A 20 minute assignment would be worth 5 points, and so on. This gives you a general rule of thumb for starting assignment points.

Most teachers know about how long particular assignments take. If I want to offer a 60 minute video with notes, that would be worth 15 points. If I assign a short worksheet which should take about 20 minutes, that would be worth 5 points. A 30 minute computer program with a short quiz at the end would be worth 10 points. And on it goes.

Using this rule of thumb, you can begin to design your first unit. Start writing down a list of objectives for the unit. Then for each objective, design two or three assignment choices for visual learners, two or three assignment choices for auditory learners, and five or six assignment choices for tactile learners. You'll notice right away that many of your assignments accommodate more than one type of learner. For example, videos accommodate visual and auditory learners. Computer programs accommodate tactile and visual learners.

Now go back and add some assignment choices for the other types of learners you have. Add at least one assignment choice for students speaking English as a second language. Add some reading assignments for students with a low reading ability. Remember, poor readers are still readers, and we want to give them opportunities to build self-efficacy on reading assignments. Try very low reading level material or assisted reading with listening centers and audio-tapes. Many publishers will also provide Spanish translations on tape for some textbooks. Inquire.

Add a couple of assignments which will be a stretch for your high ability students. Unfortunately, when trying to differentiate instruction, many teachers forget the high-ability and gifted and talented students. All students want a challenge, regardless of their functional level. This doesn't just mean higher reading level material. Add assignments which will really challenge a student during the oral defense. Have two of them provide a debate, analyze various text versions of an incident, etc.

Aim for 15 to 20 assignment choices in your "C" level. Once that is complete, build your "B" level. Here find three or four choices for students to apply, discover, or problem solve on issues you've given in the "C" level. This area is easiest to design if you brainstorm with some other teachers in your department or discipline.

The "A" level is generally easy to design. Write down a couple of topics in the unit that are currently under debate. It is especially intriguing if you can identify issues of current news. Pose the topics as questions for students to answer.

There it is, your first unit. Ready to go. Remember, don't be disappointed if it doesn't flow quite as you planned. Layered Curriculum takes some time to evolve into a workable curriculum for your particular population. But once you have something that works, the rest is a snap. Subsequent units are easy to make if you use your last unit as a template. Simply pull it up on the word processor, remove or modify activities that were not to your liking, add a few new ones, then just change the topic (remove the word "bird", replace with the word "mammal") and you're on your way.

One of the things I frequently suggest to teachers in starting Layered Curriculum is to work out your first unit, then give it to your students and tell them it is due in half the time you think it will take. For example, if you design a unit you think will take five days, tell them it is due in three days. This way, you can wait and see how things are going and on the third day, explain that you underestimated the time needed and you will give them an extra day to finish. On the fourth day you can again re-evaluate the situation and add another day if needed. This is much easier than if you gave them the expected five days to begin with and discovered it was way too much time.

I was a fantastic student until the age of ten, but then my mind began to wander. - Grace Paley

Chapter Eleven

Introducing Layered Curriculum to the Class

I f you were to walk into your classroom tomorrow and hand your students a two week unit sheet with the instructions, "choose what you want, have fun", I believe your students would be slightly overwhelmed, to say the least. Students who are unaccustomed to working in student-centered classrooms need to be instructed in how to set their own pace, find materials and plan wisely. Unfortunately, students are used to having everything mandated and spelled out for them and accepting the responsibility for their own learning may take some time.

For this reason, I recommend beginning any Layered Curriculum program with what is called a "Daily Method of Layered Curriculum". It is what I jokingly call the *training pants version*.

What you are basically going to do is walk the students through a unit using a modified whole-class instruction approach. As you can see in the example at the end of this chapter, the unit is written over my usual five day time period.

The first three days we work on "C" level assignments. I've taken the "C" level for that unit and broken it down into manageable chunks. Students must choose one assignment each day to complete, in addition to lecture notes. Students may be overwhelmed with 20 choices, but most can easily choose from three or four choices. They can also understand having to complete one assignment during the class time and most are familiar with listening to a short lecture.

On the fourth day, the entire class works on a "B" level assignment together. I walk students through the thinking process, assembling equipment, writing the lab and working it. We also go over how these assignments are graded and how to write them up.

On the fifth day, we all go to the library to work on an "A" level assignment together. Not only do they learn how to find resources, we discuss citation issues and review how to write a *good* paragraph and summary.

By the end of this first unit, all students are familiar with how the units work and are ready to do one on their own. Now, I can hand them a complete unit and they are not as overwhelmed. Occasionally, depending on the type of class, I will provide a second unit with the "C" level assignments broken into chunks again.

Following is an example of a Daily Method of Layered Curriculum from my general biology class.

The Arthropods

All 5 days: listen to the lecture and take notes. 5pts/day
1   2   3   4   5

Day 1:

1. Quietly, watch the movie. 10 pts

2. Write 15 new ideas learned in the movie. 5 pts

3. Write a 2 paragraph summary of topics covered in the video. 5 pts.

Day 2:

1. Read the chapter in any textbook on Arthropods. Be prepared to answer the end-of-the chapter questions. 15 pts.

2. On butcher paper, illustrate a poster showing the classes of arthropod and 3 examples of each. 10 pts.

3. Listen to the audio-tape and answer the questions. 10 pts.

4. Make a 4 sided paper cube. List one Class of Arthropods on each side and draw a representative of each. 5 pts.

Day 3:

1. Make a mobile for the room showing the Orders of any Class of Arthropods. 10 pts.

2. Work the computer program. 10 pts.

3. Make flash cards of the vocabulary board terms. Learn them. 10 pts.

4. Do the worksheet packet for this unit. 10 pts.

Day 4: "B" level Labs 15 pts (choose one)

1. Who jumps further, proportionately, a cricket or a human?

2. What is the average speed of an ant?

Day 5: Choose One. Use an "A" level assignment sheet.

1. Are there poisonous spiders in Utah?

2. Does the shellfish industry seriously harm natural populations of the animals?

3. Can AIDS be transmitted to humans from mosquitoes?

86+ = A   71+ = B   56+ = C   40+ = D

Chapter Twelve

Grading and Designing Rubrics

B efore giving out your very first Layered Curriculum unit, I strongly suggest making rubrics for each type of assignment you will be giving. One of the big mysteries in school for students is the grading scheme. I think they really believe we just throw darts at the board at home sometimes. Grading should not be a surprise for several reasons. First of all, people do their best when they know what is expected. Secondly, relationship building works best when expectations are clear and communication runs both ways. Thirdly, and probably most important, rubrics help take the whining out of the classroom. You know the questions, "How come she got 18 points for her picture and I only got 10?" There is no point in having to answer those types of questions. The solution here is rubrics.

Rubrics are standards or clear expectations, given up front, as to what is expected and how things will be graded. If you offer a poster assignment worth 20 points, will all posters get 20 points? Of course not. So, what does a 20 point poster look like? A 15 point poster? A zero point poster? Not only does it help the students in the work effort, in the end, rubrics save the teacher a lot of grading time as well. Once you know what a 10, 15, and 20 point poster looks like, grading is much easier.

What you want to do is write down the 10 or 15 basic types of assignments you may offer - book questions, videos, vocabulary, flash cards, computer work, posters, models, etc. Now establish on what basis they will be graded. For example, in my room I have this rubric for computer work:

> *Most of the computer programs are simple programs with self-tests at the end. They are worth 10 points. I will ask you 5 things about the program and you will get 2 points for each one you get correct. You need to have worked the program for at least a half hour.*

That's pretty clear to most students. Now they know exactly what they need to do to work the assignment and what they are expected to learn. Taking the mystery out of school will change the dynamic in your classroom. It also saves the wear and tear on your nerves from defending your grading system after the fact. I actually print these rubrics on large pieces of paper and post them around the room. As I add new assignments during the year, I add new rubrics. Some of the rubrics I use for my general biology class are found at the end of this chapter.

Grading and Grade Scales

When people first look at the grade scale I use, their first response is usually, "wow, it's so low". You can certainly make the grade scale whatever you want. Tradition seems to skew our perception of a point scale.

My initial plan was to design something that was easy to manage mathematically. Knowing that ultimately the points would end up represented as a letter grade, the points themselves were fairly meaningless. I was trying to get something that would work with the layers. I wanted the letter grade to have meaning, so I assigned the points accordingly.

A basic passing grade would entail listening to the lecture each day and doing one or two assignments. So, lecture notes were worth five points and assignments generally 5 to 15 points. A grade of "C" would indicate a basic understanding, so I would expect students to have done three to five assignments in addition to listening to the lecture.

I want a "B" to indicated higher thinking, so I cut off the "C" level work at a mathematical point that worked for my five day unit, and required the second level. The "A" level then finished off the points on a 100 point scale.

What this all means, is that teachers can assign any number of points to assignments and change the grading scale to anything that fits their school requirements or teaching comfort. The importance comes in the conversion to a letter grade, not the numerical points.

Each of my units is worth 100 points total. A minimum of 40 is required for a "D". The "C" range is 56 to 70, and the "B" range is 71 to 85. To receive an "A", the student needs at least 86 points. You could easily add pluses and minuses to any of the grades. If you cut off the "C" level at 65 points, students must complete a "B" level assignment at least to some success, in order to get the B. Without doing an "A" level assignment, a student will stop at 85 points - just one point shy of the "A".

If you have an easier way to assign points to assignments and units, by all means do it. Otherwise, this is a fairly easy system to use. Students can understand it and it's easy to calculate. I put all the points into one "pot" for the term grade, so if students are one or two points short on one unit, they can make them up on the next unit. At the end of the grading quarter, we've completed four units for a total possible of 400 points. They can divide their total by four and get their average score and calculate their own grade, as the grading scale is on the bottom of every unit sheet.

Following are Rubrics from my General Biology Class

HOW DO I DO FLASH CARDS?

Flash cards are made with plain 8.5 x 11 paper (regular size paper). Fold it in half and in half, and in half....open it up.....you should have 8 squares. Cut along fold lines to make 8 small "cards". Use 2 or 3 pieces of paper to make enough cards for the number of vocabulary words. Write the word on one side of the card. Write the definition, in your own words on the other side of the card. Learn them. They are worth 10 points.

Grading: I will choose 10 cards at random and ask you those words. You get one point for each one you know.

HOW DO I DO BOOK WORK?

Book work involves reading a section of a textbook and answering questions at the end of the reading. You may either write the answers or simply learn them in your head.

Grading: I will ask you 3 questions at random from the reading. You will get 5 points for each question you get correct.

HOW DO I DO ARTWORK?

Artwork involves posters and models. Generally they
are worth 10 points. Be creative. Artistic ability
counts in the grade.

Grade: I will ask you to tell me 5 things you've learned
in the project. Points are based on the artistic value and
the learning.

HOW DO I GET POINTS FOR MISC. READING IN SCIENCE.

You may read for at least 45 minutes on a Science topic in newspapers, magazines, books, etc. Please tell me before you begin what topic you are reading on. Upon completion I will ask you to tell me about your reading. Your summary is worth 10 points based on enthusiasm and information gained from the reading. You should be able to explain and defend 5 things you learned from the reading.

HOW DO I DO LABS?
(B LEVEL)

Labs are worth 15 points. You may only choose one lab question. It is up to you to design a procedure to solve your lab problem. Please see me before starting any procedure that involves humans or other animals. Also please see me for materials. At the end of your lab, choose one of the following ways to present your results:

1. Lab Report: A written summary that includes the questions, your hypothesis, a detail of the procedure, a discussion of what happened and your conclusion.

2. Lab Display: Using a large piece of plain paper, draw or illustrate what happened in your lab. Make sure the question is on the display and that we can see the results.

3. Lab Verbal Report: Prepare a 3 to 5 minute report containing information as in the written report in #1. See me after school to give the report or record it on audio tape.

HOW DO I DO "A" LEVEL ASSIGNMENTS?

Choose one of the A level questions. Get an "A" level answer sheet. Go to the library and find 3 recent magazine or journal articles on your topic (recent means less than 5 years).

Summarize the main points of each article. On the back write a good 2 paragraph summary of your opinion on the issue. A good paragraph contains 5 - 7 sentences. Make sure you mention some of the research when stating your opinion.

Check with the librarian if you are using articles you find on the computer database. You may need help identifying the author and magazine title from the database. These assignments are worth 20 points.

HOW DO I GET POINTS FOR COMPUTER PROGRAMS?

Most of the computer programs are simple programs with self-tests at the end. They are generally worth 10 points. I will ask you 5 things about the program and you will get 2 points for each one you get correct. You need to have worked the program for at least a half hour.

HOW DO I GET CREDIT FOR VIDEOS?

Videos are generally worth 15 points for each 45-60 minutes of video. To get those points you must watch and pay attention to the video during that time. 10 points is given for watching it and the other 5 come from you telling me about 5 things you've learned from it.

HOW DO I GET CREDIT FOR WORKSHEETS?

Worksheets are generally worth 5 points each and you can do up to 3 on any unit for a total of 15 points. I will ask you 3 questions about the worksheet and points are based on how you respond to the questions.

HOW DO I GET CREDIT FOR THE LECTURE?

Lectures are worth 5 points/day. You must be present for the entire lecture to get credit. NO EXCEPTIONS. An outline of the topic will be on the overhead and you need to copy that outline and then fill it in based on what I say during the lecture.

Mr. Knox, Now come now, come now.   You don't have to be so dumb now . . . Very well, sir, Step this way.   We'll find another game to play.
          -Fox in Socks

Chapter Thirteen

Implementing Layered Curriculum School-wide

F or all the reasons mentioned in the previous twelve chapters, Layered Curriculum like any other type of teaching method, should not be mandated by administration. Teachers, just like students, do not like things mandated. They want choice and choice leads to creativity. Therefore, the best way to implement any type of wide-sweeping change is through a slow process using a "seed" group.

To begin a school wide implementation, get a small group of interested teachers to begin designing units and implementing them in their classrooms. Make the units available through some type of in-house professional library. Ideally, you should try to get a diverse group of subjects represented. As these pilot teachers begin to share ideas and success stories with the others in the building, the idea grows.

One of the best resources for Layered Curriculum ideas will come from your special education department. When I visit with schools around the country, one of my first suggestions is to do away with special education as a separate department and integrate it into the whole school. These valuable people should be specialized in a particular discipline and then work as a member of that department. For example, in one high school I visited, there were eight special ed teachers in a faculty of 85. The special ed teachers taught a variety of subjects in self-contained classes. There was little contact between special and regular education teachers. My suggestion was to disband the special ed "department" and have each of the 8 teachers be a member of a regular education department. These special consultants would then work with the regular education teachers as advisors and creative consultants to help modify and design instructional ideas. So now the English department has a special education advisor who specializes in modifying regular English classes for diverse learners. The Science department has a special education advisor who helps design science classes and instructional education advisor who helps design science classes and instructional activities. The Social Studies department has a special education advisor, as do the technical industries classes, etc. This allows a more seamless presentation of expertise and reduces the chasm which has developed in many schools.

Schools need to make better use of their special education teachers in the regular classroom. I was visiting one school where many classes were "team taught" with a regular and special educator in the room. Many of these classrooms were not using the special education teachers to their full value. In many rooms, the special education teacher could have been confused with a parent aide. The regular ed teacher was still in control, did the direct instruction and assessment. The special educator simply monitored behavior. What a waste of a wonderful resource.

Before whole-class modifications can become a reality school-wide, the school needs to rethink the division lines between regular and special educators. First and foremost we are educators, highly trained and enthusiastic about helping children. If you erase the line between special and regular education, what you will get is extra-special education. The placement of all students in the building on a level educational playing field with opportunity and learning activities for everyone regardless of ability, disability, learning style, language, or culture.

Chapter Fourteen

Using Layered Curriculum to Increase Learning

One of the most obvious uses of Layered Curriculum is to help secondary schools implement interdisciplinary approaches to instruction, as well as provide an avenue for elementary level classrooms to build thematic units of instruction.

This book is not designed to adequately describe the advantages of interdisciplinary instruction, nor give a great detail of instruction in it, but I would like to touch on it a little. For a detailed explanation see "The Regular Educator's Guide to Interdisciplinary Instruction" by Gene Van Tassell (order information is available at the end of the book).

To really understand the advantages of interdisciplinary teaching we need to examine the workings of our long-term memory. The reference and cross-reference structure of this memory system is enhanced through this type of teaching. Let me elaborate.

Memory Systems

When we learn something, we do not learn it as an isolated free-floating factoid. We in fact learn it in the context of the setting. So, we may store the new information in categories based on a class we were in, who we were sitting with, the clothes we were wearing, the teacher, the weather, the emotions we were feeling or even the shoes we had on. We store things in our memories under categories titled "things I learned in Health Class", and "Things I learned while sitting next to Jill", and "things I learned from Mr. Patterson," or "things I think are disgusting."

In my workshops I point this out by asking participants to list all the categories they have in their memories for the word "dog" within a certain time limit. For example, we may list the category of "animals".

By category, I mean if I asked you to list "animals", you may start with elephant, lion, horse, cat, dog.... etc. So "dog" is found in the category of "animals." Other categories we'd find dog under might be *mammals, things with 4 legs, things that bark, things that smell when wet, words containing 3 letters, things with a tail* . . . and the list goes on and on.

That's the first step of memory storage - putting things in a broad category or two or three. The second step (which occurs while we sleep) is that our memory will start to cross-reference these categories. So "things with a tail" is cross-referenced with "things that bark" and "things that smell when wet." Some of the cross-referencing is done automatically, and some must be shown to us. In fact, most of the fun in learning later in life is to find new relationships or cross-references of ideas we haven't noticed before.

During retrieval of information from our memories, we will frequently access words and ideas through our cross-references in addition to the original categories. The more cross-references we have, the easier it is to access and understand an idea.

Retrieval failure in memory can often be blamed on a lack of cross-references. Most of us have had a frustrating retrieval failure on something that was not firm in our memories (usually a name of some sort). Our memories will begin to access all the cross-reference categories but we are unable to find the word. We may know that it starts with a "W" or maybe "M" and is a long word, with some double letter in it. We may even know how many syllables it has and can almost see the word, but can't get to it. This sort of retrieval failure is common with words and ideas with few cross-references. Rarely would you hear someone say, "What's the name of that animal that barks, has four legs, and smells when wet." That would seem absurd since "dog" has so many references and cross-references.

Tying this back to interdisciplinary instruction then, we can see how teaching a concept in more than one class, more than one subject, more than one perspective can help students set up cross-references in their memory systems. If students learn about early American music in history class and in music class and then study the structure of the lyric in English class, they are much more likely to remember the idea. And application of the concepts is infinitely easier with such a dynamic perspective.

Getting the school Involved

The first step to interdisciplinary instruction is generally setting up a simple matrix. This is done by having teachers of various subjects list what topics are taught throughout the year and when. After this information is assembled, the matrix can be examined to look for places where some topics overlap or places where units may be joined. Many elementary teachers are familiar with this concept in building thematic units of instruction. Layered Curriculum units lend themselves nicely to this concept.

If two or three subjects would like to try to join their topics, a unit can be designed around a common theme. The teachers could build one unit which would serve all classes, or preferably, have each teacher design a unit for his or her class and have some assignment choices overlap. Again, my suggestion would be to start small and go slowly. The first unit might be jointly designed around a common theme with only a few assignment choices in common. After the first unit, the teachers will now have a better understanding and idea of how to overlap further. Even the students may be brought in on the design process.

Another school-wide approach is to simply have some assignment choices that may involve another class. For example, having students write a poem on the Native American perspective of the European invasion on a history unit, and having it reviewed by their English teacher, would be a simple way to combine courses. You may have students write a report on the health risks of smoking for their health class, but have it typed up in the word processing class. Some assignments for science may have to be done in a foreign language and read to their foreign language teacher. With planning, teachers in both classes may offer points and a grade for the same assignment. This type of overlap does not require the same commitment as a full interdisciplinary program but may provide a good starting place for one. It certainly does help with storage into long-term memory by helping establish cross-references of information.

One of the first things school notice in adopting Layered Curriculum is improvement in end-of-the-year exams. There has been an abundance of research showing that student-centered instructional methods, like Layered Curriculum, lead to better retention for end of year tests. It is difficult to teach concepts in September that students must retain until a test in May. This is especially true in teacher-centered classrooms where learning is rather passive.

Layered Curriculum requires students to take an active part in the learning process. The fact that they choose assignments, gives students a feeling of ownership which translates in longer retention. The oral assessment also assures that learning takes place and that students have more cortical involvement during the learning process. Most of us know students who have managed to limp through school with passing grades but without much actual learning. These students are generally not held accountable for learning and can store enough information in the short term and do enough class and homework assignments that they can pass the course even without long term storage. These are the students who are going to struggle with end-of-year assessments. A student-centered approach holds students responsible for learning right from the beginning. Students learn to learn and are accountable for their learning.

Chapter Fifteen

Layered Curriculum and Brain Imaging Studies

I n the last 10 years the amount of information coming out of the neuropsychology field has been overwhelming. Unless you have been teaching on another planet for the last few years, the term *brain-based education* has come across your desk. Although the research continues to pour in and many more years will be needed to find exact applications to education, some common themes are emerging.

First and foremost is the relationship between stress and learning. Stress is the biggest obstacle in the learning process. We see stress having detrimental effects on areas of the hippocampus responsible for memory storage. We see stress effecting development of the pre-frontal cortex leading to problems with sustained attention and impulse control. We see stress early in life changing brain neurotransmitter levels, permanently, leading to low frustration tolerance and increased violence.

Memory retrieval is not possible under stress. Even the simplest of items cannot be retrieved from our memory when we feel under pressure or stress. Think back to your college days when you were desperately trying to retrieve something from your memory during a test. You knew you knew it, but you just simply could not find the information in your head. The harder you tried, the worse it became. And when did the information pop into your head?. . . the moment you walked out of the room!

Learning requires a low stress environment. Learning requires a relationship between the learner and the teacher. Higher level thinking and learning requires an environment safe for risk-taking because truly creative thinking requires risk. Creativity simply means doing, thinking and behaving different from the norm. People will not be creative if they feel threatened, intimidated or ineffective.

The needs of the world today require a level of creativity and problem solving higher than ever before. Survival in the information century require that workers are no longer just cogs in the system. Workers need to think, create, problem solve and adapt quickly. These are the skills of the higher regions of our brain. Training people in these areas requires allowing practice in using higher levels of their brain. This will not happen in an environment of intimidation and control. Intimidation and control are useful in training non-thinking workers. The traditional military model serves this purpose. Their needs were for soldiers who were trained to learn a task and obey orders without question. A creative soldier was not the goal. A military battlefield is not the place to stop and work out alternative strategy options with a superior. Many people feel the traditional military model would work well in school and perhaps it does if your goal is clean quiet classrooms full of obedient children who are trained not to think but simply follow orders. However, if your goal is to produce thinking, creative children well-prepared for the new world, this model will not be effective. Even the military is re-thinking its traditional training methods in many areas which require higher-level thinking on the part of the soldier.

Two points are clear - Number one, the brain is a use-it-or-lose-it organ. Use it and it grows and develops. Quit using it and it becomes dysfunctional and withered. Point number two, the brain's functional priorities are from the bottom up - from the more primitive to the advanced. The lower portions of the brain are wired for survival, the higher levels for thinking and creativity. In order to reach the higher levels, one has to satisfy the needs of the lower regions.

The lower regions of the brain are satisfied by having physical needs met, having safety needs met and having the perception of control. One of my colleagues is always noting that "people want to work for leaders, but manage those under them." True, and the reason for this is control. We only truly feel in control when those in superior positions over us allow us the control for our own actions and those we are responsible for, do as we say. Teachers are no different. We want freedom from administration to teach as we feel best, and students who obey our every word and are never less than perfect. But we must remember how we feel when we are managed from above. How creative do you feel when you are told exactly what to teach, when to teach it and how to teach it? There is a reason that most schools do not use packaged lesson plans. Most teachers are given some freedom in instructional design. Why? Because that freedom, or perception of control leads to more creative teaching and better cooperation in the school building. Yet, most teachers are frightened to trust that the same would be true in a classroom. How do students feel when they are told what to learn, when to learn and how to learn? Are they creative? Are they cooperative? How much better the classroom runs when students also are given some choice in their instructional design. Everything doesn't have to be completely left up to the students. They certainly are willing to work with some guidelines, just like you are willing to work with some guidelines mandated from above. But what an increase in creativity and problem solving you will see if you allow students some input in the learning process.

Meeting the Needs and Goals of Districts and States

School Boards, communities, districts and educators are very concerned with accountability, violence, diversity and preparing students for the changing economy.

One of the big cries from communities across the country is the need for accountability. State-mandated and district-mandated tests are becoming the norm. Testing and accountability are becoming key issues in the political arena. Research supports student-centered teaching methods as a way to increase long-term retention.

Layered Curriculum is one of the easiest student-centered programs to implement, particularly at the secondary level where teaching complex content to diverse learners is a challenge. Designed by and for regular educators in real-world classrooms, Layered Curriculum works with existing teaching materials and skills. With a focus on student responsibility and accountability, Layered Curriculum is a practical solution for improving test scores. In addition to holding students accountable for learning at every assignment, the "A" level assignments stress grammar, spelling, sentence structure and writing competence.

Another key concern in the education community is the apparent increase in violent behaviors in schools. Violent behaviors correlate with stress. Stress comes from the perceived lack of control over one's situation and encourages the use of more primitive regions of the brain. Teacher-centered classrooms reinforce those regions of the brain which elicit violent behavior.

Diversity in the typical classroom is overwhelming. Teachers are expected to accommodate and be sensitive to the needs of a very mixed community. Diversity can mean racial, cultural, socio-economic, gender, language, ability, political, and religious issues. More than any other modern nation, the United States seeks to educate its masses. We feel a tremendous obligation to educate everyone and as fairly as possible.

Little more than a few decades ago, education in this country was focused on the white, middle class, non-disabled child. Today our communities demand equal opportunity for all. Although this is obviously a wonderful change in attitude which we all enjoy, it presents a problem to the typical classroom teacher as teaching methods and teacher education has not always kept up with the changes in the school population. While we should celebrate the wonderful success our country has had in promoting education for all, teachers feel unprepared for their increasing role in the education of children with disabilities and the increasing cultural and social diversity issues they are asked to accommodate.

Accommodation needs to be done in the least restrictive environment and without stigmatizing anyone. Layered Curriculum places all students on a level playing field while meeting the needs of a vast variety of learners.

Layered Curriculum seeks first and foremost to engage students. It does that by providing a vast array of optional learning avenues which meet the needs of a diverse population. Even students with a history of failure discover that they can learn when allowed the freedom to learn in their own style and mode. Efficacy increases, self-esteem increases and failure rates decrease. One of the best ways to fight the increasing incidence of adolescent depression is to build self-esteem and a sense of belonging. Schools can do this by focusing on teaching philosophies which help assure a successful learning experience for all.

Chapter Sixteen

Sample Unit Sheets

H ere is one of the original units I designed for my 10th grade general biology class.

General Biology DNA & Protein Synthesis

Section I "C" level Maximum 65 points.

1. Listen to the lecture and take notes each day. (5 pts/day)
   1   2   3   4   5
2. Flash cards on vocabulary terms. 10 pts.
3. Write a paragraph on Watson & Crick's discovery of the structure of DNA. Must be done in a language other than English. 10 pts.
4. Read a chapter on DNA. Answer 5 questions
(you choose questions = 10 points. My choice = 15 points).
5. Design a creature using characteristics on board.
Write DNA sequence for him. 10 pts.
6. Find 2 newspaper articles from 1953-54 on the discovery of DNA structure. Copy and paste them on paper. Highlight important features. 15 pts.
7. Read Gene Therapy article. Answer questions. 10 pts.
8. Read Wheat article. Give an oral summary 10 pts.
9. Watch the video on DNA. Take notes and give me an oral summary. 10 pts.
10. Work the computer program on cells. 10 pts
11. Using the color code on board. Color a DNA sequence for your creature in #5. 10pts
12. Using the DNA sequence for your creature, write the mRNA, draw the tRNA and the amino acid sequence. 10 pts.
13. Work two worksheets on protein synthesis. 10 pts.
14. Find a current (this year) magazine or newspaper article on a gene discovery. Give a summary. 10 pts.

Section II "B" level Labs Choose only one 15 pts.
1. Bring in a container. Plant a seed. Chart it's growth for 2 weeks. What is it's average growth per day?
2. How do veins vary in flies? Use at least 4 different flies and a microscope.
3. How do thumb lengths vary in human adult males? (Use at least 20 subjects).

Section III "A" level. Choose only one. Use an "A- level sheet" 20 pts
1. DNA fingerprinting. Has it helped court cases?
2. Is genetic engineering in crops a good or bad thing?
3. Will the human genome project be finished on time?

Grades: 40-55 = D   56- 70 = C   71- 85 = B   86+ = A

_____   _____

parent signature/date   contact phone#
(sig. & phone worth 5 points in "C" level)

Here's a short mini-lesson.

Intro to Life Science, Biochemistry, & Cells.

Section I "C" level Maximum 65 points.
1. Listen to the lecture and take notes each day. 1 2 3 (5 points/day)
10 point assignments:
2. Flashcards on vocabulary terms.
3. Build a 3-D cell with a plastic sandwich bag. Include 12 organelles
4. Read a chapter on cells and answer 6 book questions.
5. Make a 3-D poster of two types of cells.
6. Find a newspaper article on nutrition. Give an oral summary.
7. Work the computer program on cells.

Section II "B" level Labs Choose only one
1. Can you get a seed to sprout using only water? How long will the plant live?
2. How do heart rates vary among animals? Use 3 different animals.
3. What happens to a leaf if covered in foil for 2 days? 5 days?

Section III "A" level. Choose only one. Use and "A- level sheet"
1. Exercise, Good or Bad?
2. Athletic shoes, Good or Bad?
3. Vitamin supplements, Good or Bad?
4. Dieting, Good or Bad?

Grades: 40-55 = D 56- 70 = C 71- 85 = B 86+ = A

Fish & Amphibians: Conflict and Change

Section I. "C" level 65 points MAX.

1. Write an autobiography. Include your name, age, your best physical feature, your favorite food, your favorite place to eat, describe your best friend and why, two conflicts you have in your life, where you go to feel the safest, and what you want to be doing five years from now. Write another autobiography. This time you are an amphibian. 15 pts.

2. Draw a water dwelling animal like a fish or octopus. Draw that same animal living on land. Describe the adjustments or adaptations that were made to move to land. This is an art project. It needs lots of artistic detail. Choose this only if you enjoying detailed drawing. 15 pts.

3. Watch the movie, Toadspell. Write 2 paragraphs summarizing the movie and 2 paragraphs on conflicts you saw in the movie and how change resulted from those conflicts. 15 pts

4. Listen to the lecture on amphibians. Take notes. 15 pts

5. How is a frog like a fish (list 10 similarities). How is it different (list 10 diff). Must be done in a language other than English. 10 pts

6. Listen to the lecture on fish. Take notes. 15 pts.

7. Write a 10 sentence paragraph describing the difference between frogs and toads. Read it to 2 other classmates. Your paragraph must be in a language Other than English. 15 pts

8. Find 2 pieces of conflicting information on Fish or Amphibians between two textbooks. Explain why the books may differ on information. 15 pts

9. Watch any documentary-type t.v. show on fish or amphibians. List the title and date of broadcast. Describe the show in terms of conflicts in the amphibian world. 15 pts

10. Write a piece of poetry describing either conflict or change in an amphibian's world. Get written feedback from your English teacher. 15 pts

11. Read the chapter on Fish or Amphibians from any textbook. Outline the key concepts. Be prepared to summarize your reading. 15 pts.

12. Using adding machine paper, make a time-line showing when each vertebrate class appeared on earth. You must include a scale. 10 pts.

Section II. "B" level Choose One for 15 points

1. How fast does a fish swim in MPH?
2. Which moves faster, a fish or a frog?
3. How does temperature affect fish?
4. Do frogs have taste buds?

Section III "A" level. choose ONE for 20 points

What government agencies are responsible for game fishing in our state? What environmental concerns affect that industry? Research the current role of the Fish and Wildlife Division in the State. Write a letter to your state Senator arguing either for or against the continued funding of that program.

Grading: 86-100 A 71-85 B 55-70 C 40 - 54 D

Astronomy - Earth/Moon Unit II*

100 points possible: A is 90 points B is 80 points C is 70 points D is 60 points. The student should be prepared to orally defend each project.

C Level 79 points maximum

.

1. Watch the two movies "Apollo 13" and list 10 things that were different and 10 that were the same. 20 points.
2. Draw the magnetic field of the earth and of the moon. 10 points.
3. Draw a picture of the movement of plate tectonics. 10 points.
4. List 5 things that are different in how Aristotle viewed the moon as compared to how we view the moon today. 10 points.
5. Make a table of 5 characteristics comparing the earth and moon (i.e. diameter, orbit, info, etc.) 10 points.
6. Draw the earth and moon to scale on the same piece of paper. 10 points.
7. Observe, draw, and label the phases of the moon for 4 days. 10 points.
8. Find 10 questions about the earth and moon and answer them. 10 points.
9. Flash cards for 10 vocabulary words including at least 4 describing the phases of the moon. 10 points.
10. Describe 5 things (processes, observations, etc.) Which show how the surface of the earth is different than the surface of the moon. 10 points.
11. In a language other than English, describe the difference between waxing and waning. 10 points.
12. Take a quiz on day #3 from your notes. 10 points.

B Level 10 points maximum

1. Draw, label, and understand the phases of the moon over a 2 week period.
2. Describe in detail how we can know the time by looking at the moon.

A Level 10 points maximum

Write a paper (200-400 words) using at least 3 references on one of the following issues. Take a stand and state your opinion.

1. Should we continue exploration of the moon?
2. Is there any value to the exploration of other planets and stars to those of us on earth?

*Created by and used with the permission of S. Gene Van Tassell, Granger High School, Salt Lake City, Utah.

20th Century U.S. History 1911 - 1920*

Name_____

Period_____

In the study of this decade you will be asked to do multiple assignments that will fit the six main topics (science and technology, politics, foreign policy, culture, economics, and women and minorities) that you have identified as your areas of interest. You must finish each section before beginning the following section. All work must be completed for section 1 by Thanksgiving. You will move to section 2 when we return from the break. Half the points for each task will be awarded for an oral defense of your chosen assignment, the other half will be awarded for the written assignment.

SECTION 1: Choose any of these assignments for a maximum of 140 points. You must have at least 130 points in order to move to section.

1. Write an autobiography that includes: name, address, age, parents occupation and hobbies, your hobbies, favorite food, favorite restaurant, what frightens you most, two conflicts in your life, and what you wish to be doing 5 years from now. Now write a second autobiography, this time you are living in 1916. (20 points)

2. Write a 3 page type written paper on the leadership of Tsar Nicholas II and the influence of Rasputin. (20 points)

3. Write a 3 page type written paper on the conditions of labor during this decade. Include the contributions of "Mother" Jones, "Big Bill" Haywood, Eugene Debs, and John L. Lewis (20 points)

4. Watch the movie, Titanic, then write a 1 page typewritten report on the ship itself. Then imagine your-self as a survivor, floating away in a lifeboat as hundreds of others drown. Write a letter to your mother explaining your feelings. The letter may be written in any language.20 points

5. Watch the movie, Birth of a Nation, then write a review from our social perspective of race relations, the KKK, and other pertinent events. Must be type written.(20 points)

6. Watch the movie, Eight Men Out.. Argue whether or not Shoeless Joe Jackson should be in the Baseball Hall of Fame. Be specific about what criteria you use to make your judgement. This should be in an essay format and include a clearly stated thesis. 20 points

7. Make a detailed drawing of a Mark V (male)WWI tank. Label all the elements, including machine gun, cannon, driver, continuous track, ammunition, engine and transmission, gunner, loader, commander, and frontal armor.(20 points)

8. Carl Jung and Sigmund Freud were two of the foremost thinkers in the field of psychology. Make a Venn diagram that illustrates their theories. Write a conclusion to what you find. 20 points)

9. Research George M. Cohan and his music. Present this research in a two page typewritten paper. Find at least four of his songs (must include "Over There") and play them for the class. Have the lyrics for "Over There" and after giving its background, lead the class in singing the song.(20 points)

10. Complete and define a list of at least 20 words or phrases that became popular during this decade. 20 points

11. You are a soldier on the western front in WWI. Write two entries to your diary, one from your first day on the lines, one after 6 months in the trenches. These entries must reflect the experiences of the soldier in the trenches during this war. 20 points

12. You are a suffragette. Write a speech to give before a rally that includes the President. 20 points

SECTION 2: Choose only one of these topics. There is a maximum of 30 points available. Completion of this section of the assignment will give you a B grade for this section of the class. You must complete this section before moving on to section 3.

Create a "who's who" for this decade. You must have a minimum of thirty names. You must have at least 4 people from each of the areas of study that we have identified. Each name should be followed by a short (1 paragraph) biography. There should also be a table of contents created that shows where each of your entries can be found, and under which area of study you have entered them.(30 pts)

Read Erique M. Remarque's All Quiet On The Western Front. Then watch any of the movies made with the same title. Write a review of the book, then a written critique that compares and contrasts the movie with the book. In your paper include a conclusion on which was more powerful.(30 pts)

Read War Games by Michael Foreman. Find the Garth Brooks song (Belleau Wood) that deals with much the same subject. Present an oral review of the book to the class, present the Garth Brooks song, and then lead the class in singing "Silent Night".(30 pts).

Construct a wall map of Europe in 1914 and another for 1919. Make sure that your details show the changes brought about by WWI. These maps must be at least 3 X 6 ft.(30 pts)
This section must be turned in by December 3. Everything must be typewritten.

Section 3: Choose only one of these topics. There is a maximum of 30 points available. Completion of this section of the assignment will give you an A grade for this section of the class.

Read George Orwell's Animal Farm. Since it is an allegory for the Russian Revolution, assign the animal characters their "proper" names and actual roles played in that event. Give some historical background on each character and provide a brief, typewritten review on how well Orwell did in depicting the Bolshevik revolution in such a unique manner.

Write a six page, typewritten research paper on any one of the following artists: Nijinsky, Duncan (Isadora), Picasso, Matisse, Ravel, or Debussy. Provide visuals to show the work of your chosen subject.

Write a six page, typewritten research paper on any one of the following athletes: Jim Thorpe, Ty Cobb, or Jack Johnson. Provide charts or graphs comparing their abilities and exploits to modern athletes.

Research the mystery of "Anastasia". Watch the Ingrid Bergman film of that name. Include in your research the claims of Anna Anderson of Charlottesville, Virginia and the findings of the scientific tests done on the mass grave site in 1989. Write a five page, type-written report on your findings and your conclusions.

Created by and used with the permission of Daniel Rideout
Salem-Keizer Public Schools, Salem, Oregon

U.S. History 1921 – 1930*

Name_____Period_____

In the study of this decade of our history, you will be asked to do multiple assignments that will fit the six main topics (science/technology, politics, foreign policy, women/minorities, culture, and economics) that you have identified as the areas of your greatest interest. You must finish the required work in each section before you move to the next set of choices. Section 1 will be finished by January 14. You will receive half the available points for each task for the written work and half from an oral defense of what you have learned doing that task.

Section 1: Choose any of these assignments for a maximum of 140 points. You must have at least 130 points to move to section 2.

1. You have been charged with bootlegging. You have an opportunity to defend yourself in either oral or written form. If you choose the written format, it must be a traditional 5 paragraph essay that will meet the state CIM standards (to be used as a work sample). If you choose to defend yourself orally, again state CIM standards will be used. It must be at least 5 minutes in length (to be used as a work sample). (20 pts)

2. Draw a "Picasso" portrait. See me for the directions on how to do this! (20 pts)

3. Draw or create a "disassembled" model of Henry Fords Model T. Give detailed directions on how to assemble your model based upon Ford's assembly line technique. This must make technical sense (for instance you would not attach the steering wheel before you added a steering column). (20 pts)

4. Research the rise of the KKK during this time period. Write a two page typewritten paper on the differences in the Klan during this decade and in the decade following the Civil War. Include a conclusion of why you think the Klan had a resurgence and why it took the shape that it did. (20 pts)

5. Watch the movie Matewan. Write a two page typewritten paper on the plight of the coal miners and how organized labor (unions) helped or hurt them. (20 pts)

6. Participate in Mr. Gordon's stock market game for 10 rounds. You will keep a stock portfolio and records of all your transactions. Bonus points may be earned with exceptional performance on your stock portfolio. (20 pts)

7. Make a collage of the fashions of this decade. Watch the movie Thoroughly Modern Millie. Write a one page typewritten paper critiquing the costuming of the movie. This of course may be a positive or negative critique. (20 pts)

8. It has been said that every Blues singer had their own definition of the "blues" (i.e.: "Blues aint nothin' but a good man feelin' bad", "Blues is a cryin' woman whose man's gone and left her"). Listen to a complete album of Ledbelly, and Bessie Smith. Come up with your definition of the blues, and in a one page typewritten paper give both your definition and a defense of that definition. (20 pts)

9. Jazz was very big in the 20's. Listen to a complete album of Ella Fitzgerald or Louis Arm- strong and an album of George and Ira Gershwin. All are considered to be great "jazz" musicians but the music is much different. In a two page, typewritten paper review the musical merits of each, explain what is different, and speculate on why there are such differences. (20 pts)

10. Watch any one of the movies, "Inherit The Wind". Using the information from the movie and from research, write a two page typewritten report on what happened (and why!) to John Scopes. (20 pts)

11. Present to the class at least 5 Langston Hughes poems. Explain who he was and how he came to write what he did. (20 pts)

12. Write a letter to Marcus Garvey that either attacks or agrees with his "back to Africa" proposal. It must include at least two historical references to events in Garvey's life. This letter may be written in the language of your choice. (20 pts)

13. Research the "red scare" of the 20's and the Palmer raids. Write a two page, typewritten paper on why the country suffered from such paranoia during this time. (20 pts) .

14. Do the section review questions from Chapter 20 in the Addison Wesley book. (20 pts)

Section 2: You have completed the tasks necessary to move to the "B" level of this unit. Following are 4 tasks. You are to choose only one. It must be completed and in to me by Friday, January 21. Maximum points on this section is 30.

1. In 1923 Robert Goddard began testing on a rocket. To honor his research and his contribution to both rocketry and NASA, you are to build a "bottle rocket". You are limited only by good sense (this((the rocket-not your good sense)) will be tested outdoors) and your fuel, which must consist of vinegar, water, and baking soda. Any other fuel will automatically disqualify you from receiving any points. You must also have a two page typewritten paper on Goddard and his research and contributions. (30 pts)

2. During the 1920's it took 13 days to drive from Oregon to New York City. I want you to do a "AAA" style "trip tick". You must provide road maps (from the roads available during this decade), where you intend to stay, average miles per day, average miles per hour (you are driving the very latest Model A in 1929), where you will have to gas up (you must know both the mpg and size of the tank for a Model A), and a budget for the trip. Your budget will have to provide the costs of your budgeted items from 1929. That information can be located in our library. (30 pts)

3. In 1927 John Gutzon de la Mothe Borglum began his sculpture of Mt. Rushmore. You are to provide a two page typewritten paper on this monumental task, and of Borglum's background. You are also to duplicate his finished Mt. Rushmore, to scale, using whatever materials you choose. (30 pts)

4. There were numerous dance crazes during this decade, but perhaps none more popular than "The Charleston". You and a partner may demonstrate this dance to the class, and teach them to do at least some of

the basic components of this dance. I have the music if you do not. (27 pts/30pts if in the dress of the time)

Section 3: Congratulations. You are now at the "A" level of this unit. Of the four tasks that follow, you are to choose one. It is to be completed and turned in to me by Friday, January 28. Your maximum point total for this section is 30.

1. "Widespread use of the automobile more permanently altered the socio-economic structure of this country than any other event of the first half of the twentieth century". You are to assess the validity of this statement using at least five areas of criteria. Please clear these areas with me prior to beginning your research. (30 pts)

2. Research any one of the following sports heroes: Jack Dempsey, Helen Wills, Lou Gehrig, Babe Didrikson, or Babe Ruth. Complete a six page, typewritten research paper on your subject. In addition, provide pictures and comparative statistics to a current star in the sport(s) in which your subject excelled. (30 pts)

3. Perhaps nothing is more closely linked to the "Roaring 20's" than Prohibition. Provide a research paper on Prohibition that includes a brief history of the Temperance movement, the political and social implications of this experiment in control of social behavior, and how it is linked to "organized crime". It should be at least six typewritten pages in length, but you are likely to have more! (30 pts)

4. Research the phenomena known as the "Harlem Renaissance" and write a six page, typewritten paper on the subject. It is to include not only examples of the work and opportunities that this "renaissance" provided for writers and artists, but also the social conditions that existed in Harlem and the problems that were created from success. (30 pts)

*Created by and used with the permission of Daniel Rideout Salem-Keizer Public Schools, Salem, Oregon.

What is a Mineral?*

"C" Requirements
Listen to lecture/take notes daily 5 pts/day M T W TH F
Flash cards on vocabulary terms (see handout) 10 pts.
Read chapter/answer questions Sec 1,2, and 3 5 pts. each section
Read article and answer questions. 5 pts.
Watch video/give oral summary or take notes 10 pts.
Work on computer (website) and answer question at the end. 10 pts.
Work on worksheets daily 2 pts. each
Cut and fold to make shapes 10 pts.
Locate minerals around the house and make a list. 5 pts.
Use WAS to plan deadlines for projects 5 pts.
Draw how minerals are formed using figure 10-5 with explanation 5 pts.
Find magazine article related to minerals, copy, and highlight important parts. 5 pts
Research your state in regards to minerals and draw map. 10 pts.

"B" Requirements
Lab Activity: Growing synthetic gemstone or crystal garden/summary 15 pts.
Lab Activity: Mineral Hardness/summary 15 pts.

"A" Requirements
Research activity using references (see handout) 20 pts.
Design poster or slide show using the earth's crust, mineral groups, mineral properties, and hardness of minerals. must include description and examples of each layout. 20 pts.

*Created by and used with the permission of Meg Vickers, Great Mills High School, Maryland.

Geometry - Area

Goals:
Find the area of basic plane figures
Find the surface area of 3-dimensional shapes

"C" level work (72 points max)
____Take notes for each lesson. (5 pt each): Day 1, 2, 3, 4
____Book assignments done correctly and completely for full credit
pg 246;1-17all (10 pt)
pg 248; 1-20all (10 pt)
pg 245;1-12all & pg250;1-11all (10 pt)
pg 258; 3-9all & pg 261; 3-9all (10 pt)

Other assignments (10 pt each)
____On graph paper, draw 5 different parallelograms. Find the area of each by counting squares, then find the area using A = bh.
____Cut out two sets of 1 inch squares. Have 12 squares in each set. Paste each set so that they make two different rectangles of 12 sq inches in area. How many more other sizes of rectangles can be formed?
____Map handout
____Home activity handout
____Newspaper handout
____Make a poster of 5 different triangles with area of 36 sq inches
____Draw 4 circles of radius 1 unit, 2 units, 3 units, and 4 units on graph paper. Find the areas of each by counting squares, then find the areas using A = r.
____Make a poster of the steps to find the area of a circle with diameter 10 inches.
____Problem 13 on page 245, problem 19 on page 251
____Draw the net (flat layout) of two prisms and two cylinders and create a 3-dimensional model of each.
____explain in your own words, how would you find the surface area of a prism and a cylinder.
____Make a cylinder out of grid paper and calculate the surface area by counting squares, then find surface area using SA = 2 r + 2 rh.
____Do unit quiz 8A

"B" level work. Choose only one (10 pt)

____Take the unit test with a score of 72%
____Circle handout with at least 7 correct
____Surface area handout (soda can)
____Performance assessment of score 2

"A" level work. Choose only one (10 pt)

____Give an oral presentation (or video) with drawings on how to find the   areas of the shapes covered in this unit.
____Performance assessment II with a score of 5.
____Building construction handout

*Created by and used with the permission of Jerry Schaffer, Bonneville Jr. High, Salt Lake City, Utah.

Geometry*

Goals:
Basic geometry terms
Angles
Polygons

C" level work (70 points max)
_____Take notes for each lesson (5 pt. Each) Day 1, 2, 3, 4, 5, 6
_____Book assignments. Done neatly and completely for full credit.
Pg. 212; 1-28 all (5 pt)
Pg. 214; 1-12 all & pg. 216; 1-15 all (5 pt.)
Pg. 220; 1-12 all (5 pt)
Pg. 224; 1-19 all (5 pt)
Pg. 226; 1-25 all (5pt)
Pg. 228; 1-20 all (5 pt)
_____Identify each piece of a Tangram puzzle. Using all seven pieces make a parallelogram and a rectangle. Draw a diagram of where each piece needs to be. (10 pt)
_____Lab activity 2.6 handout (10 pt)
_____Calculator activity 7.7 handout (10 pt)
_____Perspective drawing handout (10 pt)
_____Activity on pg. 211. Get handout (10 pt)
_____Make a poster with each of the definition terms (in bold type) on Pg. 212. Have a drawing of each definition with appropriate labeling for each. Also, include a description of each term in your own words. (10 pt)
_____Find ten things in your home that have an angle. Describe each and how the angle is formed. (10 pt)
_____Make a poster that describes how to measure an angle. Have a drawing for each step. (10 pt)
_____Newspaper activity handout (10 pt)
_____Newspaper activity handout (10 pt)
_____Home activity handout (10 pt)
_____Make up three word problems that contains two acute angles that when added equal 90 degrees. (10 pt)
_____From a newspaper or magazine, find three examples of acute angles right angles, and obtuse angles. (10 pt)

_____Make a poster that contains representations of parallel lines, skew lines, and perpendicular lines. (10 pt)

_____Make a poster that describes all classifications of triangles based on sides and angles. (10 pt)

_____Make a poster that is a family tree for the family of quadrilaterals. Include a description and picture of each quadrilateral. (10 pt)

_____ Take the unit quiz. (10 pt)

"B" level work. Choose one (10 pt)

_____Take the unit Test with a score of 72%.

_____Alternative assessment with a score of 2 or better.

"A" level work. Choose on (10 pt)

_____Write a paragraph on each of the geometric shapes and relationships that has been covered in this unit that you see from the time you wake up until you get to school. (10 pt)

_____State three ideas form this unit that show up in real life. Write an explanation for each one that describes why you chose it and where is found in the real world.

A 90-100, B 80-84, C 68-72, D 54-58

*Created by and used with the permission of Jerry Schaffer, Bonneville Jr. High, Salt Lake City, Utah

8th Grade U.S. History
Constitution of the United States*

Section I "C" Level Maximum: 415 points.
Do all of the following for a total of 345 to 355 points.
1. Do the Work Sheets each day.   (5 pts. each x 33 work sheets = 165)
wk 1   wk 2   wk 3   wk 4   wk 5   wk 6
2. Do the Bell Work each day.   (5 pts/day x 30 days = 150 pts.)
wk 1   wk 2   wk 3   wk 4   wk 5   wk 6
3. Memorize the Preamble:
* Write it once perfectly   (10 pts)   or
* Say it perfectly before the class   (20 pts)
4. Keep Constitution Notebook NEAT and in ORDER.   (10 pts)
5. Keep Syllabus Outline up-to-date.   (5 pts)
6. Keep Unit Sheet Checklist current.   (5 pts)

Choose from the following to earn 25-60 pts.
7. Listen to lectures and discussions and complete the notes, outline, etc., as directed. (5 pts each)
8. Watch the Schoolhouse Rock video - "The Preamble"- and compare (tell the similarities and the differences in) the words of the song and the Preamble in the Constitution. (5 pts)
9. Watch the Schoolhouse Rock video - "I'm Just a Bill" - and write a summary. (5 pts)
10. Make a poster to illustrate the six goals of the writers of the Constitution.   (10 pts)
11. Do a current event project on one of the following: Legislative Branch, Executive Branch, Judicial Branch, the President's Cabinet, or another topic related to the Constitution or the federal government (check with teacher first on the last one). May do a maximum of two from #11. (10 pts)
12. Explain to the teacher the system of checks and balances.   (10 pts)   (+5 pts if you explain to the class.)
13. Draw a detailed flow chart of "How a Bill Becomes a Law".   (10 pts)

14. Use a poster to illustrate five of the most important amendments, five freedoms in the Bill of Rights or the five basic freedoms in the 1st amendment. (10 pts)

15. Use a chart to compare the two US presidents who have been impeached. (10 pts)

16. Build a model of one of the following buildings or monuments in Washington, D.C.: the White House, the Capitol, the Washington Monument, the Lincoln Memorial, or the Jefferson Memorial. (10 pts)

17. Do a collage featuring pictures of current congressmen, the president, federal judges, cabinet members, etc. (10 pts)

Section II   "B" Level   Maximum: 50 points

Do a research paper on one of the following:

1. A biography of one of your states' Senators or the Representative from your area.

2. The president's cabinet. Include their names and what each cabinet member does.

3. A Biography of one of the members of the Constitutional Convention in 1787.

Section III   "A" Level   Maximum: 50 points

Choose one of the following:

1. Write and present a three- to five-minute play demonstrating the five basic freedoms of the Bill of Rights.

2. Propose an amendment, based on research of a problem, and take it through the steps involved in becoming a law.

3. Choose a current events issue, research the pros and cons, then take a side and support your opinion based on your research.

Grades: D = 320-369   C = 370-419   B = 420-469   A = 470-525

Note: These grades for the Layered Curriculum unit on the Constitution will count for 70 % of your total grade on the Constitution. The tests will be count for the other 30%.
Parent Signature   Contact phone #

*Created by and used with the permission of Janet Winters, Tropico Middle School, Rosamond, California.

7th grade circulatory system*

Name:_____Chapter 3 Period:_____

The Circulatory System   Objectives:

1. Explain the role of the circulatory system.
2. Compare an open versus a closed circulatory system
3. Describe the path of the blood through the heart, lungs, and body.
4. Compare arteries, veins, and capillaries.
5. Explain what causes a pulse.
6. Explain how the blood moves through the body under pressure.
7. Compare the structural adaptations of blood vessels.
8. Compare the circulatory systems of various animals.
9. Describe the role of fatty deposits in the heart.
10. Relate lifestyles to increased blood pressure.

Sunshine State Standards:

Strand F. Processes of Life 1. The student describes patterns of structure and function in living things. Benchmark SC.F.1.3.1 - 7.01
Strand H. The Nature of Science 1. The student uses the scientific processes and habits of mind to solve problems. Benchmark SC.H.1.3.5 - 7.01, SC.H.1.3.6 - 7.01
3. The student understands that science, technology and society are interwoven and interdependent. Benchmark SC.H.3.3.4 - 7.01, SC.H.3.3.5 -7.01 and SC.H.3.3.7 - 7.01

Section 1 "C" Level Select activities equaling 750 points

__1. Participate in the lesson daily. (10 points/day)
__2. Explore Activity and Written Report (choice of 3)- 50 points each
__3. Find Out Activity and Report (choice of 3)- 50 points each
__4. Chapter Questions pp. 90, 101, & 105 - 100 points
__5. Chapter Review Questions p. 111 - 100 points
__6. Multi- Cultural Connections Activity - 50 points
__7. Concept Map - 25 points
__8. Study Guide - 100 points
__9. Take Home Activity and Report - 50 points
__10. Transparency Worksheet (choice of 4) or other worksheet (choice of 2) - 25 points each
__11. 1 Paragraph description of he circulatory system in any language other than English. 50 points
__12. Scientific Drawing Label Diagram of the Circ. System 50 points

___13. How it Works - 25 points
___14. Chapter Review Worksheet - 25 points
___15. Critical Thinking Activity (choice of 3) 50 points each
___16. Parts of me Poem - 25 points
___17. Flashcards - 25 points
___18. Video - 50 points.
___19. Circulatory System URL - 25 points

Section 2 "B" Level - Select activities equaling 150 points
___1. Making Connections - Integrating Science 50 points
___2. Exploring Further - Design Experiment and give Oral
Presentation 100 points
___3. Making Connections Across the Curriculum 50 points
___4. Making Connections - Technology and Society 50 points
___5. Video - Fantastic Voyage - 100 points.
a. chronological journal of the voyage
b. evaluation of the accuracy of the description
___6. Skills Assessment - 50 points
___7. Investigate Activity and Report (choice of 2)- 100 points each

Section 3 "A" Level - Select activities equaling 100 points
___1. Bulletin Board describing the benefits of proper diet and
exercise with a week long plan for diet and exercise. 100 points
___2. Display comparing circulation in a plant cell compared to an
animal cell. 100 points
___3. Create a Holmes Scale for Teens 100 points
a. Survey 30 teens with the scale
b. Graph the results
c. Present orally
___4. Create a Power Point Presen. of the circul. system. 100 points

Grades: 650 - 749 = D, 750 - 849 = C, 850 - 939 = B, 940 - 1000 = A

***Created by and used with the permission of Carol Anderson, Ft.
Meyers, Florida**

Environmental Science*

Per.: _____ Name:_____
Air Pollution Unit-10 class periods
Due: End of class, Feb 14th Total Points _____ Letter grade:____
Objectives:
Examine the types, causes, and sources of air pollution.
Demonstrate and observe results of smog and acid rain on plants and objects.
Recognize dangers of smog and acid rain and to the environment and determine solutions.

To get a "C" in this unit, get at least 70 points from a combination of any of the projects in the A, B, or C categories:

____ ____ ____ ____ Listen to and take notes on the lectures--5 points per day

____ ____ ____ *** Read a section of the text, take notes--5 points each

____ ____ ____ Listen to the chapter sections on tape. Take notes--5 points each

____ * Make 25 flashcards for chapter vocabulary on note cards or quia.com--10 points

____ * Write 20 quiz or jeopardy questions and answers on note cards or quia.com -10 points

____ * Make a chart showing types and sources of air pollution--5 points

____ ____ Copy or print a brief (2-3 page)article on air pollution, its health effects, or acid rain OR * read one of the provided articles. Take notes or write a summary on the back--5 points each

____ Observe the results of someone else's experiment ,discuss it with them, take notes--5 points

____ Interview someone who treats people suffering from the effects of air pollution, bring in a transcript of your interview and your conclusions--10 points Permission from teacher ____

____ * Write a paper (one page) defending one side of "Is it better to prevent or clean-up air pollution" with 3 supporting reasons and one source --5 points

____ * Make a poster showing in detail how acid rain &/or smog is formed--10 points

_____ * Draw and color a world map showing areas most effected by acid rain--5 points

For a "B" you must do at least one of the following and have a total of 85 points:
_____ * Write and perform (privately to Ms Cook, publicly to the class, or on video) a skit (3+ minutes), poem, or song (16+ lines) about the effects of air pollution or acid rain--10 points

_____ _____ * Design and perform an experiment that shows the effect of acid rain on statues. OR Perform experiment * 6.1, * 6.2 (requires seven day observation period), 6.3 (in class only, requires five days observation and previous arrangements), OR an approved equivalent. If done outside of class, supervising adult must sign your lab report. Write up a lab report--10 points

For an "A" you must earn 15 points by doing of the following and have a total of 95 points:
_____ * Read and summarize (max. ½ page each) three current magazine or Internet reports (of at least 3 pages in length each) on one topic concerning air pollution, its health effects, or acid rain. Add an 8+ sentence paragraph giving your opinions or conclusions based on the facts in the articles. In addition to your paragraph, list 5+ ideas as to what should be done &/or is being done to reduce air pollution and its effects. Copy the articles and attach your summaries, paragraph, and list and turn in as one packet.

*Created by and used with the permission of Janet Cook, Japan

Here's an example where the "C" level is broken into specific days for students who want more structure. They still need to find time during the 5 day unit to work on the "B" and "A" level if that is where they are headed.

Mammals

Section One 65 POINTS MAX
Day 1
1. Take notes from lecture 5 pts.
2. Make 15 flashcards from Terms on Board. Learn them. 10 pts.
3. Write a one page overview on the Class of Mammals. List 2 sources. 10pts.
4. Make a color picture representing various types of Mammals. 5 pts.
xxxxx
Day 2
Choose an Order of Mammals _____. (no duplicates/class)
1. Read and summarize 3 articles from Ranger Rick on your Order. 10 pts
2. Write 1 page overview of your Order. list 2 sources. 10 pts.
3. Make a color picture representing various members of your Order. 5 pts.
4. Watch the laser disk on your Order. Write 15 new things about its members. 10 pts
5. Make 10 flash cards of Scientific/Common Names of member of your Order. 10 pts
xxxxx
Day 3
Choose a Family within your Mammal Order. _____.
1. Read the section in Holt on mammals. Be prepared to answer the review ques. 10pt.
2. Write a 1 page overview of your Family. List 2 sources 10 pts.
3. Make a color picture representing various members of your Family. 5 pts.
4. List 15 animals who are members of your Family. 5 pts.

Day 4

1. Choose a specific species of mammal. _____.

2. Write a ´ page report on their habitat. 5 pts

3. Write a ´ page report on their reproduction/child rearing. 5 pts.

4. Write a ´ page on environmental concerns regarding your animal. 5 pts.

5. Make a color picture showing your species in its habitat. 5pts.

xxxxx

Day 5

1. Watch the video. List 15 mammals found. 5 pts

2. List the scientific name of 5 of the mammals. 5 pts.

3. List the Order of 10 mammals found in the video. 5 pts.

4. Give a 2 minute (max) oral report on the Order/Family/ or Species from this unit. 10 pt

Section Two 15 POINTS MAX - Choose one only

1. What type of Mammal was eaten by a barn Owl? Dissect a pellet and reconstruct the
skeleton.

2. How is a bat skeleton similar to a whale skeleton? Draw each and compare/contrast
them.

Section Three 20 POINTS MAX - Choose one only

Find 3 recent magazine articles on the topic. List and summarize EACH
article and write a paragraph of your opinion.

1. How did nearly all the marsupials end up in Australia?

2. What can be done to save the Manatee?

3. Besides humans, what is the most intelligent mammal?

Grades: 86+ A 71+ B 56+ C 40+ D

General Biology Viruses

Name_____ Period_____ Due Date_____

Section I "C" level Maximum 65 points.
1. Listen to the lecture and take notes each day. (5 pts/day)   1   2
    3   4   5
2. Flashcards on vocabulary terms. 10 pts.
3. Write a paragraph on the discovery of the polio vaccine. Must be
done in a language other than English. 10 pts.
4. Read a chapter on viruses. Answer 5 questions (you choose
questions = 10 points. My choice = 15 points).
5. Design 4 viruses attacking 4 different cells. Include RNA and
DNA structure. 10pts.
6. Find 2 newspaper articles from the 1950's or 60's explaining new
vaccines. Copy and paste them on paper. Highlight important
features. 15 pts.
7. Read one of the xeroxed articles_____. Give an
oral summary 10 pts.
8. .Read one of the xeroxed articles_____. Give an
oral summary 10 pts
9. Watch the video on viruses. Take notes and give me an oral
summary. 10 pts.
10. Write a children's book about Sue, the lysogenic virus and Tom,
the lytic virus.10 pts.
11. Work two worksheets. 10 pts.
12. Find a current (this year) magazine or newspaper article on an
oncogene discovery. Give a summary. 10 pts.

Section II "B" level Labs Choose only one 15 pts.
1. Interview someone with a lytic virus. Get a 3 day account of
symptoms (objective and subjective). Hypothesize about what stage
the virus is in each day.
2. Interview someone who has had cancer or lived with someone with
cancer. Find out how the virus progresses, treatments and how the
disease affected the person and family..
3. Design an experiment for testing a new AIDS vaccine. Include
number of trials, subjects, and length of study.

**Section III "A" level. Choose only one. Use and "A- level sheet"
20 pts**

1. Will we have a vaccine for AIDS in your lifetime?
2. Is the chicken pox vaccine a good idea?
3. Why is Utah last in the nation for vaccinating our children?

Grades:
40-55 = D   56- 70 = C   71- 85 = B   86+ = A

_____   _____

parent signature/date   contact phone#
(sig. & phone worth 5 points in "C" level)

Grapes of Wrath*

Name:_____.
 Parent's signature adds 5 pts to Level "C":_____
"C" Level: **6** points each. Maximum "C level" is 65 points
(Includes lectures that are **4** points)

1. Find the latitudes and longitudes (Hint: see *Rand McNally Classroom Atlas*): Pocatello, ID Enid, OK   Sioux Falls, SD Greeley, CO   Acapulco, Mexico   Gadsen, AL   Devil Lake, ND Shelby, MT (estimate the answers between two lines)

2. Copy the part in *Grapes of Wrath* that tells why Grandma tricked the agricultural inspector.

3. Copy the city names and write the states that they are in: West Palm Beach,   Suffolk,   Salt Lake City, Miami,   Las Cruses, Atlantic City,   Reno,   Mesa   (Don't write on this paper.)

4. In *Grapes of Wrath* who were the "Okies"? Why did they come to California? Why were they treated so badly in California?

5. Draw a picture of the Government Camp in *Grapes of Wrath*. How was it different from the private camps?

6. During WWII military tanks needed gas, oil, and water. How are these used in tanks? Why is it important to control the supply of gasoline in warfare?

7. Compare the maps of both Cuba and the Philippines in American's Journey, pg. 642. What do these maps tell us about the amount of fighting in Cuba vs. the Philippines?

8. Who was (1) Adolph Hitler (2) Benito Mussolini (3) Hirohito?

9. Look up "Child Labor". Write: How are the kinds of work that kids do today different from the kinds of work that kids did in the 1800s and early 1900s. Why aren't the jobs the same now as then?

10. Draw or write about what the camps were like in *Sent Away*, the book about Japanese relocation.

11. In the book *Sent Away*, write about what happened to the people, and why it happened.

12. Answer the geography questions in *Skills for School Success*, page 45.

13. What two or three things do you think that grownups worried about when they were young? What do grownups worry about today?

14. When it comes to worrying how are kids today like their parents? Written --or done as an interview between you and a partner. (Has to go about 2 to 3 minutes if you do it as an interview-discussion.)

"B" Level. Choose only one. (Each one is 15 points, but do only one.)

Research and find out about President Roosevelt's Executive Order 9066. List your source. Explain how this could happen again. How many people were involved? Typed.
Define "punishment". Define "reward". If you want somebody to do something, which is better, punishment or reward? Explain and use examples from *Grapes of Wrath*. Name another case in history when people were punished. Explain. Typed.

"A" Level. Choose only one. 20 points maximum.
Define Oath (not meaning using bad words). Describe the Loyalty Oath in *Sent Away*. List two or more sources (titles and authors). Do you believe that loyalty oaths are good to have? If you do, then write your own loyalty oath. If you do not, then explain why and list several good reasons to support your belief. Typed, one and a half pages.

Think about the Japanese Relocation in WWII. Take the part of one of the people who were moved: what do you have to say about it. Then take the part of President Roosevelt and tell what he has to say about it. Lastly, what are your feelings about the Relocation? Typed, one and a half pages.

*Created by and used with the permission of Gilbert Gia, Stiern Middle School Bakersfield City School District

The Changing Planet*

Name:_____ Due Date:_____

Section I "C" Level Maximum 70 points.

One of the C level activities may be completed in a language other than English.

Required: Listen to lecture and take notes every day. Write a reflection paragraph using the writing prompts given to you to record your learning from the lecture. 10 pt.

Answer Science Log questions # 1-4, pg. 452. Sentences must be complete and you must write the questions in your science notebooks. 5 pts.

Make flashcards on vocabulary terms: geologist, geology, volcanologist, Mesosaurus, Pangaea, tectonic plates, crust, mantle, lithosphere, asthenosphere, and core. 10 pts.

Pretend you are a travel agent. Design a poster to get your clients to visit the scenic landscape of your choice. Your poster must have a title, a picture of the landscape, and at least a paragraph at the bottom that describes to the reader the highlights and most appealing thing about the place you chose. It also must include geological conditions and facts. Pg. 454 will help with this assignment. 15 pts.

Answer questions #1-6, pg. 456. You must write the questions and answers must be in complete sentences.

Use the Continental Jigsaw Puzzle worksheet and follow direction on pg. 459. You will have to cut out the 6 major landmasses and glue them together to from one super continent. When finished you must complete the letter started on pg. 459 to the Geological society on why you think the continents where once joined. Use your super continent as proof in the letter. 15 pts.

Use the discussion debate on pg. 460 from the Royal Geological Society. In your science notebook make a T-chart and label one side FOR ant the other side AGAINST. Read the purple discussion and list comments made that support Wegener's idea of Pangaea under the FOR side and comments made against his ideas under the AGAINST side. 10 pts.

Make a model of the earth's layers. You may use clay or any other creative materials to show the earth's layers. Be prepared to discuss each layer and its purpose. 15 pts.

Answer the "Seven Major Plates and Their Movement" questions #1-6 on pg. 465. You must write the questions and answers must be in complete sentences.

Study the 5 stages in the breakup of Pangaea. In your science notebook draw how future plate movements might change the geography of the world. 10 pts.

Explain Island Hot Spots and explain letters a-d in your discussion. Pg. 468 #1. 10 pts.

Do Geologic Time Tape. Construct a geologic time line that will show major geologic ears, periods, epochs, and organisms. Use Geologic Time Tape worksheet. 10 pts.

Write a humorous story using the science vocabulary words from C level #3. 10 pts.

Make up an imaginary conversation between the earth's layers. 10 pts.

Do a KWL chart about geology, the earth, or earthquakes. 10 pts.

Record a music tape and call it The Music of the Earth. Record sound of the earth's rotation, movement of tectonic plates, convection currents, etc. Be creative and be able to explain the meaning of each sound. 15 pts.

Collect magazine photographs of landforms. Organize the photos into sequential order or group them by related phenomena, such at the development of a river valley or a coastline. For each group of related images, write a few words to identify or explain the processes occurring. 10 pts.

Ask and expert a question about geology that you have been curious to know. Use the Internet. Go to my web site at geocities.com/pino1972 , scroll down to science links and click on Ask and Expert. Click on Ask-A-Geologist, and send your question through the Internet. Print out the reply. 10 pts.

Watch the video, "Hell's Crust". Tell me at least 5 things that you learned from the video. You may take notes when watching the video. 15 pts.

Section II "B" Level All assignments are 15 pts.

Choose only one Lab Experiment. All experiments must be completed in the Scientific Method. For help on the Scientific Method, visit my web site at geocities.com/pino1972 and click on the scientific method. All lab experiments must have a report written in Scientific method, a Lab display, and lab verbal report.

How do convection currents contribute to the movement of tectonic plates? Include the Thinking it Over questions in your conclusion. Complete experiment on pg. 462.

How are the layers of the earth similar to a sandwich? Use worksheet guide provided.

What is the Mantle like? Use worksheet guide provided.

Which is a better model of the earth: a softball, a silly putty egg, a globe, or a hard-boiled egg? Use worksheet guide provided.

Section III "A" Level All assignments are 15 pts

Choose only one assignment. Include a bibliography page of your resources and cite them correctly.

Earthquakes affect the economy, architecture, and many other aspects of life in regions near the plate boundaries you have learned about. Scientists estimate that hundreds of small earthquakes occur every day and that larger and more dangerous earthquakes are always a possibility. As a result, cities located in tectonically active areas, such as the Pacific Rim, have special building codes and other laws that are designed to minimize earthquake damage. Do research on the architectural and economic impact of earthquakes on an area, Some possibilities to investigate include costs required to make a building earthquake-safe and architectural strategies for earthquake-resistant buildings.

The Mid-Atlantic Ridge rises above water at only one place. Iceland. Find Iceland on a map and indicate the Arctic Circle, which includes the northern part of the island. These two features indicate that Iceland is a place of both extreme cold and extreme heat. Do some research on what life is like in Iceland. Make sure to focus on how geologic processes, such as glaciers, geysers, or volcanic activity, affect the lifestyles of the people who live there.

Life around spreading zones on the sea floor, where molten rock flows onto the sea floor from the Earth's interior, is different from life anywhere else on Earth. Ordinarily, food chains of living things depend on energy from the sun. However, the creatures that exist around these deep-sea zones (called hydrothermal vents) receive energy from chemicals in the water. Research how hydrothermal vents occur and what organisms exist around them.

Grades: 0-49 =F 50-59 =D 60-70 =C 71-85 =B 86-100=A

Parent Signature/Firma de Padres Phone #/Numero de teléfono

(Signature and phone number worth 5 points in "C" level.)

Created by and used with the permission of Priscilla Pino, Pueblo Del Sol Middle School in Phoenix, AZ.

October Sky*

If you want a D

1. Be in class each day. Be on time. Stay awake. Watch the movie. 5pts each day

2. Write one page or 100 words giving your opinion of the movie. What did you like What didn't, you like? (Does not need to be typed, but must be done neatly.)

Day1 - Day 2- Day 3 - Day 4 -

If you want a C

All five assignments are required.)

1. Watch the movie each day. don't sleep don't do work for other classes. (5pts each day)

Day 1 - Day 2- Day 3- Day 4-

2. Fill in an outline sheet for 3 days. this must be turned in at the beginning of class the next day. (You may skip one day. or do one more for extra credit*) (5pts per day)

Day 1 Day 2 Day 3 Day 4

3. Writing Assignment- What do you think the American Dream is: Interview two other people and find out what they think. Take notes turn notes in with your rough draft. Write 150-200 Words discussing your ideas and the ideas of the two people you talked to. Have one other person proofread for you. (Fill out partner proofreading for m and hand in.) We will type and print the final copy in class. (15pts)

4. Choose one topic for your homework assignment. (15pts)

Locate one source of information about the topic you choose. (Encyclopedia, book, magazine, Internet, newspaper, etc.) Read the information, take notes, write down the information for your bibliography. You may then choose to write 1 page - to 100 word report to show me what you learned. No credit is ever given for plagiarism! your paper does not need to be typed, but must be neat, proof read and correct all mistakes. (partner Proofreading form) OR you may choose to make an illustration (drawing, cartoon, collage, etc.) Showing something you learned from your research. Be prepared to explain what you learned to Mrs. Beggar by the due date above.

You must still include notes and a bibliography that is done correctly. (All artwork must be Neat, colorful and recognizable, and at least 8x11" paper or larger. Do not use lined notebook paper for your artwork.)

TOPICS (just choose one)

Sputnik

Werner Von Braun

5. Library Assignment. You may look for your source for your research, look for a book for your book report or read. Fill in the assignment. 5pts.

If you want a B:

Complete all of the assignments required for a C and then choose two assignments below. For each assignment you may either write 150-200 words, (Must be neat and be sure to correct all mistakes. You may type it if you wish , but don't have to.) Or you may show ideas through artwork. Be prepared to explain your illustration and ideas to Mrs. Biggar by the due date. 15pts You cannot get a B with out doing one of these assignments.

1. Discuss the relationship between homer and his father. Use specific examples from the movie compare their relationship at the beginning of the movie and then at the end.

2. Miss Riley says that sputnik means that things will never be the same again. What do you think she means? Do you agree?

3. Retell one important scene in the movie from the point of view of one of the other boys, not Homer.

4. Pretend you are Homer. Give advice to someone who is thinking of dropping out of school, or someone who thinks school isn't very important.

6. Describe a situation where you have had to use something you learned in a math class.

7. Describe something you learned in a science class that you can relate to your life, or that you have used in some way.

8. Make an illustration of one important setting from the movie. Explain why this place is important.

9. Draw a picture of one important character. Write two paragraphs about this person.

10. Design a costume for one of the characters. Explain why this person would wear this. What does the way they dress reveal about their personality and what is important to him or her?

11. Explain why you think Homer became so fascinated with rockets.

12. Take notes on the improvements that Homer and the other Rocket Boys make on their rockets. (At least 10) Explain why each improvement was or wasn't important to their final success.

13. Make a list of 10 things that Homer had to learn in order to succeed in achieving his dream. Explain why he needed to know each thing that you list.

14. Why is the coal mine so important to homer's father? How are Jahn and Homers dreams and goals the same? (or are they?)

15. Discuss the differences and similarities between teenagers today and teens in 1957. Use specific examples from the movie and from your observations of teens today.

16. relate an experience you have had where you achieved something in spite of great problems, or succeeded in something that other people thought you could not do. How did you overcome the difficulties you faced? What happened?

17. Write a poem (10 lines or more) expressing the feeling of one of the characters, or about something that happened in the movie.

18. Find 5 newspaper articles that you think show something about how the American Dream is happening or not happening for people in America today. Cut out the articles, read them carefully. For each article write a short summary of the article, then explain how each article relates.

If you want an A:

Complete all of the required assignments for a C and one B assignment. Then choose one assignment below. ALL A ASSIGNMENTS MUST BE TYPED DOUBLE SPACED. Be sure to correct spelling and grammar mistakes. Be sure your sentences and paragraphs are correct. (20pts) all a papers must be at least 200 words unless otherwise specified.

You cannot get an A without doing one of these assignments.

1. Watch the video The Right Stuff ". Compare it to the movie October Sky.

2. Create a survey to get information about social groups at Granger High School and the different attitudes towards athletes and students who excel academically. Survey at least 20 students. Explain what you learned. Include your surveys with your paper.

3.Compare what you think each of these characters would say that The American Dream means to them: Homer, John , Jim ,Elsie. Use specific examples from the movie that would support you opinions. Compare to your dreams for the future.

4. Research the importance of coal mining in American History. Find at least 2 sources Summarize what you learned. Would your research support what Jahn Hemkham says in the movie if coal fails and if steel fails American fails.

5. Think of an invention that you think would make life at school or life in general, easier. Draw a diagram of your invention and write at least 100 words explaining what it is and who it works.

6. Find a copy of the book The Rocket Boys by Homer Hickham. Read it and write a comparison with the movie. What is the same? What is different? what is your opinion of the book?

7. Teach a concept to our class from your current math or science class. Use visual aids. Explain it in a way we can understand, and show us why this is an important thing to understand and be able to use.

A=90-105 B=90-100 C=65-79 D=36-64 D-=35

Created by and used with the permission of Terry Biggar, Salt Lake City, Utah.

Mama exhorted her children at every opportunity to 'jump at de sun.'
We might not land on the sun, but at least we would get off the ground.
. -Zora Neale Hurston

Chapter Seventeen

A collection of Teaching Tips

This chapter really should have been titled a potpourri of miscellaneous ideas that didn't fit anywhere else, but that title was too long.

If you are working with students **preparing for Advanced Placement** and other tests of that type - insist they are tested in your classroom. Cue-triggered recall is a major memory asset. Students are put at a disadvantage when tested in an environment foreign to the one they were in while learning.

Too many **students quitting at the "C" level** in your Layered Curriculum units? Make sure your "B" level activities are enticing. Try assignments that involve food, live animals, or other atypical class activities. The "B" level choices should pull your students.

Thank your students every day, individually, for coming. Too often, students go from the beginning of the school day to the end without anyone recognizing the fact that they got up, dressed, and came to school. For many children, just getting to our classroom was a remarkable accomplishment.

Remember, **testing material** falls into the category of "unassisted reading material" and therefore should be written AT LEAST two full grade levels BELOW a student's level of reading. This is different than a textbook reading level. If a textbook is written at an "8th grade reading level" this means that 50% of 8th graders can comprehend it with teacher assistance. Obviously you don't want to use this level for unassisted exam material.

When making **"A level" assignments for younger children** (or even older children) have them use people rather than library research material for their references. They can get opinions on their topic from 3 different adults (or 3 different 5th graders or 3 different teachers, etc.). Have them summarize the 3 opinions, either orally or on paper, and then form their own opinion.

Have students who write well in a foreign language **translate units sheets** for you. You can keep these in a file to use throughout the year when you get new students who struggle with English but speak/read a different language. It allows them to be engaged in a learning activity right away.

Layered Curriculum works particularly well in **summer school** programs where you may have condensed time-frames for course objectives. Offering a variety of assignment choices gives students more freedom and the perception of control which encourages more out-of - class learning and work.

Those **"nature sounds" CD's** that are available everywhere make nice noise monitors in the room. Turn it down low and it tends to calm students and the noise level. In my room it helps monitor the noise level as well because when students get too loud, I just say, "hey, I can't hear the birds" (I use the rainforest CD).

January is the **peak month for S.A.D.** - seasonal affective disorder --depression caused by decreased melatonin levels. Generally high in the winter because melatonin is produced by sunlight. In your classroom, open the shades, or if you are in a room with no windows, use incandescent light bulbs (regular screw-in type from home) to add to the light in the room. Flourescent light does not increase melatonin levels.

Research tells us that an **effective classroom** is based on student opinion, not teacher opinion. Poll your students from time to time. A simple evaluation I frequently use poses only 3 questions: what should I keep doing?, what should I start doing?, what should I stop doing?

In **math assignments** offer both book work and worksheet problems. Many children, especially those with ADHD, struggle with book work simply because they have to transfer the problems onto their own paper. They get lost, confused, and make copy errors.

Model appropriate behavior. This is especially important in situations where you are angry and upset. You can teach all the conflict resolution curricula you want, but students learn most by watching you. Remember, you may be the only person in their life who models appropriate behavior when angry.

Use cue-triggered recall to help students study for major exams. Have them wear a special shirt or outfit while studying and then wear the same outfit during the test.

Offer your lecture time as an option - you'll probably have more students listen.

Use caution when doing fund-raisers so that you are not exploiting your students. Ask yourself: are these students raising funds for an issue they feel is important and immediate to their needs (ie: a field trip, cage for the class hamster, save the park) or are they motivated by extrinsic rewards offered by the fund raising company (pizza party for winning class, trip to Disneyland for top selling student in the district, etc.?) Too often fund raisers involve using child labor to benefit an out of state company in order to raise money for a general educational issue such as technology or books for the library. These items are the responsibility of the taxpayers, not the children. In addition to exploiting our students, these practices encourage children to work for extrinsic rewards rather than intrinsic ones.

Inservice your students on Layered Curriculum and brain biology. Take the first day to teach your students the hows and whys of your teaching methods. A simple concept, but one that will make your teaching so much easier. Once students understand why you are asking them to do something, they are much more cooperative.

Color code those unit sheets. The simplest, yet most effective way to help with organizational skills.

Spend a significant amount of time early in the year working on **building a relationship with your students.** Real learning involves risk-taking and people are more likely to take risks in an environment they trust.

Treat every child like you would like your own child treated by his/her teacher.

Make sure you include students in **setting the classroom rules**. When students show up for day one and the rules are already posted, students lose that perception of control which can lead to behavior problems.

Remember the heat factor. **The brain requires an immense amount of water** to function properly. This becomes especially important in learning and especially difficult in hot classrooms. Encourage water bottles if possible or allow water breaks frequently.

Children who have any type of **auditory processing difficulty** often have increased problems in the beginning of the year. Allow even more time after asking questions until students get used to your voice and the novel visual distractions in a new room.

Try something new. Throw out the laminated lesson plans (or at least file them) and freshen your approach to teaching. Even if it is not something you continue all year, it may give you a little boost in enthusiasm for teaching again.

Color code things in the room. Instructions, folders, period files, subjects, etc. Color is wonderful in assisting with administrative skills (for teacher and student).

I washed me face and hands before I come, I did. - Eliza Doolittle.

Appendix A:

Research for Further Reading

Here are some of the more interesting "hot topics" which have been covered in the Help4Teachers newsletter.

Florida Atlantic University made a comparison study of student adjustment problems during the transition between elementary and middle school. The study compared learning disabled students with students without learning disabilities. Interestingly, the study found no difference in school adjustment problems during the transition. Good or bad, students with learning disabilities tend to fare just as well as students without learning disabilities.

Forgan, and Vaughn (2000). Journal of Learning Disabilities, vol 33(1), 33-43.

The Journal of Educational Psychology published a study showing how teacher gestures can improve student problem-solving strategies, particularly in math. If teachers did not gesture at all or gestured differently than the strategy conveyed by speech in explaining a problem, students later showed less understanding than students whose teachers used hand gestures which matched and supported the verbal explanation.

Goldin-Meadow, et .al. (1999). Journal of Educational Psychology, vol. 91(4), 720-730.

Anthony Pellegrini at the University of Minnesota has a new article in the current issue of the Journal of Educational Psychology on school bullies and victims. The study of 5th graders shows 14% of them are bullies, 18% are victims. Bullying was negatively correlated to peer popularity. Being liked by classmates was found to be a protective factor against being a victim of bullying.

Pellegrini (1999). Journal of Educational Psychology, vol. 91(2), 216-224.

Columbia University has released a study showing a strong relationship between anxiety and poor memory ability -The relationship is particularly strong in young boys at risk for delinquency.

Pine, et al. (1999). Journal of American Academy of child and Adolescent Psychiatry, vol. 38(3), 1024-1031.

A study out of Germany shows that early detection of hearing impairment is possible by listening to a baby's cry. "Expert listeners" can detect hearing impairment and its severity through melody, perceived sound, and rhythm of the cry.

Moller, et. al. (1999). Speech and Communication, vol. 28(3), 175-193.

Gordon Millichap at Northwestern U Medical school has published documentation which accuses Methylphenidate as a possible cause of Tourettes syndrome. Among other studies, Millichap shows the strong correlation between Methylphenidate (ritalin) and the increase in Tourettes.

Millichap (1999). Developmental Medicine & Child Neurology, vol. 41(5), 356.

The University of Pennsylvania has exposed another gender difference in human brains. They show that women have a greater percentage of gray matter whereas men have a higher percentage of white matter. Men have equal percentages of white matter in both hemispheres, but a greater amount of gray matter in the left hemisphere than right. There was no difference in hemispheres in women. (White matter is made white by myelination which speeds up electrical flow.) The higher percentage of grey matter in women's brains is thought to allow more area available for computation to make up for the overall smaller cranial space in the skull. (white matter is thought to allow transfer of information across distance).

Gur, et. al. (1999). Journal of Neuroscience, vol.19(10), 4065 - 4072.

Good news from the Washoe Sleep Disorders Clinic in Reno, Nevada (a good place for a sleep disorders clinic if you ask me). Short-term sleep deprivation does not impair cortical function. While it has been shown many times that long term sleep deprivation interferes with test taking, attention and task completion, apparently sleep deprivation for shorter periods of time do not.

Binks, et.al.(1999). Sleep, vol. 22(3), 328-334.

Dartmouth medical school is using MRI imaging to show that there is a structural difference in the brains of people with dyslexia. In particular, they've found an area of the perisylvian region (associated with language) called the caudal infrasylvian surface (CIS) which is significantly larger in the brains of persons with dyslexia.

Green, et. al, (1999). Neurology, vol. 53(5), 974-981.

The Rockefeller University released interesting findings on hippocampus damage due to stress. Apparently stress, both acute and chronic, suppress growth of dendrites and neuron maintenance in the hippocampus region specific to episodic and semantic memory. It is not clear whether the cell loss is permanent or a "reversible atrophy".

McEwen (1999). Annual Review of Neuroscience, vol. 22, 105-122.

A University of Michigan study found a positive correlation between help-seeking behavior and student's perception of classrooms which address their social and emotional needs. A longitudinal study of middle-schoolers shows that children tend to ask for help in classrooms where the emphasis was on trying hard, making self improvement, and had an environment where risk-taking was allowed. In classrooms where relative ability and criteria goal setting was emphasized, students were less likely to seek help. It should also be pointed out that this help-seeking behavior was unrelated to the teacher's view of the classroom, only the students' view.

Ryan, et.al,(1998). Journal of Educational Psychology, vol.90(3), 528-535.

The brain area responsible for circadian rhythms (suprachiasmatic nuclei) is analyzed in a new study out of the University Catholique de Louvain in Belgium. The study also describes the strong relationship between depression and sleep disturbances, especially REM depravation.

Eilien, et.al. (1999). Irish Journal of Psychological Medicine, vol. 16(1), 18-23.

A study at the University of California helps shed new light on the problem of seductive details in text. Seductive details are illustrations or funny stories which are designed to catch and keep student attention, but generally end up shifting their focus so that they do not grasp and retain the main intent of the text. Many studies have shown that students have lower test scores on information presented in text with seductive details than in straight texts which simply lay out the information. According to this study, the placement of the seductive details is important. These extraneous stories and pictures do the most damage when placed at the beginning or dispersed throughout the passage. They do the least damage when placed at the end. Does this mean we need to get rid of textbooks with interesting stories, funny tales and exciting illustrations? Probably not, as we know students are more likely to read when the text holds their attention, but we need to make sure that the stories and illustrations are not irrelevant in providing content ideas, otherwise they become distracting. Too often the students remember only the dramatic, irrelevant pictures and not the main idea being presented.

Harp & Mayer,(1998). Journal of Educational Psychology, vol. 90(3), 414-434.

Appendix B:

Glossary of Special Ed Categories

Although by no means an exhaustive list, these are the disabilities most often seen in the regular classroom. For further information on accommodating specific disabilities in the regular classroom, see "The Regular Educator's Guide to Special Ed" available at http://help4teachers.com.

Attention Deficit and Attention Deficit/Hyperactivity Disorder (ADD/ADHD)

A student diagnosed as ADD or ADHD has a neurological disability. It affects about 5% of the general population, or 1 in every 20 students, males are more frequently affected. When inattention includes hyperactivity, the child's diagnosis is ADHD. Many children have inattention without hyperactivity. They have ADD. There may be a genetic component to ADD causing it to run in families. However, many prenatal and postnatal factors have also been linked to ADD/ADHD.

Parts of their brain, especially the frontal lobes which handle planning and attention, have a chemical imbalance which limits blood flow and functioning. This makes it difficult, even impossible, to focus attention on the important stimuli in the room (like the teacher) and ignore the unimportant stimuli (like the fan noise).

Students with ADD have been successful in school through a combination of three types of interventions: structure in their learning environment, formal behavior management programs, and the use of stimulant medication (such as Ritalin) to normalize brain function.

Autism and other Pervasive Developmental Disorders (PDD)

Students with pervasive developmental disorders, such as Autism, Rhett's and Asperger's syndrome, have severe problems with social interactions and an extremely narrow field of interest and activities, making peer relationships difficult. Language and other communication skills are usually severely impaired. The majority of these persons have mental retardation, but some high functioning persons are able to attend school in regular classrooms.

These students often have severe auditory processing problems which means they cannot process what they hear quickly enough to understand verbal instruction. This may be intensified somewhat by an unfamiliar voice so it is particularly difficult toward the beginning of the school year. These students typically do not interact much with other students, and group projects and discussions will be challenging. Any type of change is particularly difficult for students with PDD.

Communication Impairments

Students with a communication impairment have speech that interferes with their ability to communicate. They may have trouble formulating, expressing, receiving, or interpreting oral language. Students with receptive language deficits experience difficulty comprehending oral language such as class instructions and lectures. Students with expressive language problems may understand oral instructions but may experience difficulty retrieving words and organizing their thoughts to be understood by others.

Emotional Disturbance (ED) and/or Behavior Disorder (BD)

Students with an emotional disturbance may show inappropriate behavior and feelings. Their ability to learn may be hampered by depression or general unhappiness. They may have difficulty with interpersonal relationships and demonstrate aggression or anxiety.

These students may also appear withdrawn and are often reluctant learners. They are frequently absent or tardy. They may be confrontational and challenge authority. Students with emotional disturbances are easily frustrated and often have incomplete work.

Fetal Alcohol Syndrome

Fetal Alcohol Syndrome and Fetal Alcohol Effect shows itself in both physical and mental disabilities. In addition to nervous system problems and deficiencies in growth, persons with FAS may have facial abnormalities, and are frequently mentally retarded as well. Their attention span is short and memory systems impaired. These students need definite structure to the school day and work best within very small time constraints and meeting short-term goals. Teachers need to be consistent, brief in instruction and persistent.

Gifted and Talented (GT)

Although not a disability, giftedness is considered an exceptionality and should be taken into consideration in the regular classroom. Specific criteria for giftedness varies from school district to school district, but generally includes a combination of IQ score and academic achievement. These students generally need approaches to learning that involve organizing, processing, and managing information in a divergent manner.

Learning Disabled (LD)

A student labeled as LD, or learning disabled, has difficulty processing information. They may struggle with one or more of the following: language, memory, listening, speaking, reading, writing, spelling, math or motor skills that cannot be attributed to their intelligence level. LD is a large category of students with **normal intelligence** who fail in school. This means that IQ tests and other types of testing indicate that the student *should* be able to do some task which they are unable to do or have difficulty doing. They have a problem with storing, processing and/or producing information which is reflected in the way they receive and express information. Learning disabilities range from mild to severe.

Included in this category are students with dyslexia, dyscalculia, and dysgraphia. These students have problems with reading, math, and writing, often due to language development problems. To be categorized as learning disabled the student must have *at least* average intelligence, with a measurable difference between their potential and their performance in an academic area. Some may be gifted students in one or more areas. These students *can* learn, but need material presented in a different modality or form than the traditional classroom offers.

Tourette's Syndrome (TS)

Tourette's syndrome is a category of tic disorders. Unlike other types of tic disorders, Tourette's is a life-long disability. The tics accompanying this disorder may change over time in both complexity and frequency. A person with Tourette's has both motor and vocal tics. These rapid, apparently purposeless movements may include eye blinking, facial tics, throat clearing, yelling, barking, coughing, spitting, touching themselves or others, arm flapping, obscene phrases, or stuttering.

Appendix C

References, Research and further Reading

I f you still need some "hard research" to back up your efforts in implementing a student-centered program, here are some references which you may use in presenting your ideas to colleagues, administration or district people

Research Supporting Student-Centered Instruction

Benware & Deci 1984. The quality of learning with an active versus passvie motivational set. American Educational Research Journal, 21, 755-765.

Boggiano et al., 1993. Use of techniques promoting students' self-determination: Effects on students' analytic problem-solving skills. Motivation and Emotion, 17, 319-336.

Deci, Schwartz, et al., 1981. An instrument to assess adults' orientations toward control versus autonomy with children: Reflections on intrinsic motivation and perceived competence. Journal of Educational Psychology, 73, 642-650.

Deci & Ryan, 1987. The support of autonomy and the control of behavior. Journal of Personality and Social Psychology, 53,1024-1037.

Deci, Nezlek, & Sheinman, 1981. Characteristics of the rewarder and intrinsic motivation of the rewardee. Journal of Personality and Social Psychology, 40, 1-10.

Flink, et al, 1992. Children's achievement-related behaviors: The role of extrinsic and intrinsic motivational orientations. In A. K. Boggiano & T.S. Pittman (Eds.), Achievement and motivation: a social-developmental perspective (pp. 189-214). New York: Cambridge University Press.

Grolnick & Ryan, 1987. Autonomy in children's learning: An experimental and individual difference investigation. Journal of Personality and Social Psychology, 52,890-898.

Koestner, Ryan, Bernieri, & Holt, 1984. Setting limits on children's behavior: The differential effects of controling versus informaitonal styles on intrinsic motivation and creativity. Journal of Personality, 52, 233-248.

Patrick, Skinner, & Connell, 1993. What motivates children's behavior and emotion? Joint effects of perceived control and autonomy in the academic domain. Journal of Personality and Social Psychology, 65, 781-791.

Reeve, 1996. The interest-enjoyment distinction in intrinsic motivation. Motivation and Emotion, 13, 83-103.

Rigby et al., 1992. Beyond the intrinsic-extrinsic dichotomy: Self-determination in motivation and learning. Motivation and Emotion, 16, 165-185.

Shapira, 1976. Expectancy determinants of intrinsically motivated behavior. Journal of Personality and Social Psychology, 34, 1235-1244.

Valleran, Fortier, & Guay, 1997. Self-determination and persistence in a real-life setting: Toward a motivational model of high school dropout. Journal of Personality and Social Psychology, 72, 1161-1176

References & Research

Allis S. (1996, November 4). The struggle to pay for special ed. Time, p.82-84.

Atwater, M. (1995). The multicultural science classroom. The Science Teacher,60(4), 40.

Bradford, P. (1993). The first step in learning is learning to feel good about yourself. In R. Jennings (Ed.), Fire in the eyes of youth: The humanities in American education (pp. 79-86). St. Paul, MN: Occasional Press.

Bradley, D. & West, J. (1994). Staff training for the inclusion of students with disabilities: Visions from school-based educators. Teacher Education and Special Education, 17,(2), 117-128.

CH.A.D.D. (1996). Children and adults with attention deficit disorders. Ch. A.D.D. Online! Available online at: http://www.chadd.org/.

Chiras, D. (1992). Teaching critical thinking skills in the biology & environmental science classrooms. The American Biology Teacher, 54(8), 464-468.

Collins, M. (1993). Origins. In R. Jennings (Ed.), Fire in the eyes of youth: The humanities in American education (pp. 25-37). St. Paul, MN: Occasional Press.

Dalheim, M., (Ed.). (1994). Toward inclusive classrooms. National Education Association of the United States Teacher-to-Teacher Series. Washington, DC: NEA Publications.

Darling-Hammond, L. & McLaughlin, M. (1995). Policies that support professional development in an era of reform. Phi Delta Kappan, 76(8), 597-604.

Dempster, F. (1993). Exposing our students to less should help them learn more. Phi Delta Kappan,74(6), 432-437.

DeWijk, S. (1996). Career and technology studies: Crossing the curriculum. Educational Leadership, 53,(8), 50-53.

Dunn, R. (1990). Bias over substance: A critical analysis of Kavale and Forness' report on modality-based instruction. Exceptional Children,56, 352-56.

Dunn, R., Beaudry, J., & Klavas, A. (1989). Survey of research on learning styles. Educational Leadership,46(3), 50-58.

Evers, R. & Bursuck, W. (1994). Literacy demands in secondary technical vocational education programs: Teacher interview. Career Development for Exceptional Individuals, 17,(2), 135-143.

Fuchs, L., Fuchs, D., Hamlett, C., Phillips, N., Karns, K. (1995). General educators' specialized adaptation for students with learning disabilities. Exceptional Children, 61,(5), 440-459.

Fuentes, K. & Weinberg, P. (1993). New York and the world. In R. Jennings (Ed.), Fire in the eyes of youth: The humanities in American education (pp. 1-13). St. Paul, MN: Occasional Press.

Fullan, M. (1994). Change forces: Probing the depths of educational reform. Bristol, PA: Falmer Press.

Glaser, R. (1990). The reemergence of learning theory within instructional research. American Psychologist, 45(1), 29-39.

Glynn, K., Rajendram, K. & Corbin, S. (1993). Perceptual-based student outcomes assessment process in the marketing curriculum. Journal of Education for Business, 69(1), 11-18.

Good, T., & Brophy, J. (1991). Looking in classrooms (5th ed.). New York: Harper & Row.

Harris, J. (1995). Sheltered instruction. The Science Teacher, 62, 24-27.

Guild, P. (1989). Meeting students' learning styles. Instructor, 99(8), 14-17.

Hollowood, T., Salisbury, C., Rainforth, B., Palombaro, M. (1994). Use of instructional time in classrooms serving students with and without severe disabilities. Exceptional Children, 61,(3), 242-253.

Houck, C. & Rogers, C. (1994). The special/general education integration initiative for students with specific learning disabilities: A "snapshot" of program change. Journal of Learning Disabilities,27,(7), 435-453.

Inclusive Education: A series of issue papers. (1994). Illinois Coalition on School Inclusion, Springfield. (ERIC Document Reproduction Service No. ED372 525).

Janney, R., Snell, M., Beers, M., & Raynes, M. (1995). Integrating students with moderate and severe disabilities into general education classes. Exceptional Children, 61,(5), 425-439.

Katz, J. (1996, May 11). Policy on disabled is scrutinized over discipline problems, cost. Congressional Quarterly Weekly Report, p. 1295-1299.

Keegan, M. (1995). Psychological and physiological mechanisms by which discovery and didactic methods work. School Science and Mathematics, 95(1), 3-10.

Lewis, R. & Doorlag, D. (1995). Teaching special students in the mainstream (4th ed.). Englewood Cliffs, New Jersey: Prentice Hall.

MacAuley, D. & Johnson, G. (1993, Summer). Behaviorally disordered students in mainstream settings: A pedagogical-interactional perspective. Teacher Education Quarterly, 87-100.

Manning, M. & Lucking, R. (1990). Ability grouping: Realities and alternatives. Childhood Education, 66(4), 254-258.

Moore, C. (1993). Twelve secrets of restructured schools. Education Digest, 59(4), 23.

National Education Goals Report: Building a nation of learners. (1994). US Government Printing Office. Washington, DC.

Nunley, K. (2000). In defense of oral defense. Classroom Leadership (ASCD). February.

Nunley, K. (1996). Going for the goal. The Science Teacher, September.

Putnam, J., Spiegel, A., Bruininks, R., (1995). Future directions in educational inclusion of students with disabilities: A delphi investigation. Exceptional Children, 61(6), 553- 576.

Rainforth, B. (1992). The effects of full inclusion on regular education teachers. A report to California Research Institute on the integration of Students with severe disabilities. San Francisco State University. (ERIC Document Reproduction Service No. ED365 059).

Rankin, D., Hallick, A., Ban, S., Hartley, P., Bost, C. & Uggla, N. (1994). Who's dreaming? -- A general education perspective on inclusion. Journal of the Association for Persons with Severe Handicaps,19,(3), 235-237.

Renzullli, J., Reis, S. & Smith, L. (1993). The revolving door identification model. (Available from Creative Learning Press, Inc. P.O. Box 320 Mansfield Center, CT. 06250).

Renyi, J. (1993). The arts and humanities in American education. In R. Jennings (Ed.), Fire in the eyes of youth: The humanities in American education (pp. 1-13). St. Paul, MN: Occasional Press.

Sanchez, G. (1993). This hard rock. In R. Jennings (Ed.), Fire in the eyes of youth: The humanities in American education (pp. 105-113). St. Paul, MN: Occasional Press.

Schrag, J. & Burnette, J. (1994). Inclusive schools. Research Roundup,10,(2). A publication of the National Association of Elementary School Principals.

Schultz, J. (1994). Inclusion: The debate continues. Instructor, 104,(4), 55-56.

Schultz, J. & Carpenter, C. (1995). Mainstreaming Exceptional Students: A guide for classroom teachers. (4th ed.). Boston: Allyn & Bacon.

Schumm, J. & Vaughn, S. (1995). Getting ready for inclusion: Is the stage set? Learning Disabilities Research and Practice, 10,(3), 169-179.

Seal, K. (1993). Performance-based tests. Omni, 16(3), 66.

Smith, S. (1993). Enabling the learning disabled. Instructor,103,(1), 88-91.

Sperling, D. (1993). What's worth an "A"? Setting standards together. Educational Leadership, 50(2) 73-75.

Tindal, G., Rebar, M., Noet, V. & McCollum, S. (1995). Understanding instructional outcome options for students with special needs in content classes. Learning Disabilities Research & Practice,10(2), 72-84.

US Department of Education. (1991). Thirteenth annual report to Congress on the Implementation of the Individuals with Disabilities Education Act. Washington, DC: U.S. Government Printing Office.

Vann, A. (1993). Let's get the curriculum reform train off the bell-curve track. Education Digest, 59(1), 32.

VanTassel-Baska, J. (1988). Developing scope and sequence in curricula. Gifted Child Today,11(4), 58-61.

Vaughn, S., and others. (1994). Teachers' view of inclusion. Paper presented at the Annual Meeting of the American Educational Research Association. New Orleans, LA, April 4-8, 1994. (ERIC Document Reproduction Service No. ED 370 928).

Weaver, R. L. (1990). Separate is not equal. Principal, 69(5), 40-42.

Wigle, S. and Others. (1994). Full inclusion of exceptional students: Three perspectives. Paper presented at the annual meeting of the Mid-Western Educational Research Association. Chicago, IL, October 12-15, 1994. (ERIC Document Reproduction Service No. ED 377 635).

Willis, S. (1995, Summer). Reinventing science education. Curriculum Update (Supplement to Education Update) Association for Supervision and Curriculum Development.

Wilson, S., Peterson, P., Ball, D. & Cohen, D. (1996). Learning by all. Phi Delta Kappan, 77(7), 468-476.

Wlodkowski, R. & Ginsberg, M. (1995). A framework for culturally responsive teaching. Educational Leadership, 53(1), 17-21.

Yasutake, D., Lerner, J., Ward, M. (1994). The need for teachers to receive training for working with students with attention deficit disorder. B.C. Journal of Special Education, 18(1), 81-84.

Yatvin, J. (1995). Flawed assumptions. Phi Delta Kappan, 76(6), 482-484.

Index

Additional information, lesson plans and ideas are available at:
http://Help4Teachers.com

Additional books, guides and workbooks
ORDER FORM

3 Ways To Order:

1. Go to: http://Help4Teachers.com/books.htm

2. Fax this form to (801)253-4603

3. Mail this form to:

Help4Teachers
9699 South 2810 West
South Jordan, UT 84095

___Layered Curriculum: The practical solution for teachers with more than one student in their classroom. $19.95

___Layered Curriculum: WORKBOOK $12.00

___The Regular Educator's Guide to the Brain $10.00

___The Regular Educator's Guide to Special Ed $5.00

___The Reg. Educator's Guide to Special Ed - parent's edition $8.00

___Keegan: Looking at the world through Autism $5.00

U.S. shipping/handling $2.50 1st book ($1.25 each additional book)

Total # books:_____ Total amount including shipping $_____

Visa/Mastercard #_____exp.date_____

Name on Card:_____

(in case of problems) daytime phone(_____)_____

Shipping address:_____

_____

_____

_____

Workshops, Presentations and Keynote addresses are available.
Email: kathie@brains.org